William Ewart Gladstone

Landmarks of Homeric Study

Together with an Essay on the Points of Contact between the Assyrian Tablets and

the Homeric Text

William Ewart Gladstone

Landmarks of Homeric Study
Together with an Essay on the Points of Contact between the Assyrian Tablets and the Homeric Text

ISBN/EAN: 9783337231194

Printed in Europe, USA, Canada, Australia, Japan

Cover: Foto ©Thomas Meinert / pixelio.de

More available books at **www.hansebooks.com**

LANDMARKS

OF

HOMERIC STUDY

TOGETHER WITH

AN ESSAY ON THE POINTS OF CONTACT BETWEEN

THE ASSYRIAN TABLETS AND THE

HOMERIC TEXT

BY THE

RIGHT HON. W. E. GLADSTONE

London

MACMILLAN AND CO.

AND NEW YORK

1890

CONTENTS

SECTION I

THE HOMERIC QUESTION

I

By the use of the term Homerology, I desire to mark the fact, that the study of the Homeric text is not like the examination of an ordinary literary record. That text covers the whole field of human experience for what may be called an organic period in the rise of a most important race, and includes the delineation of an age. This field of history is more limited, without doubt, as to time, than Egyptology or Assyriology, considered in each case as the study of the respective monuments. But it is far more minute and diversified in its presentation of human life, experience, character, and thoughts. It is in

Œ   B

effect, therefore, as I contend, to be treated as a
distinct branch of ancient science.

II

Apart from all literary uses and enjoyment of
the Poems, that separate and early age of human
history, to which they introduce us, is one of
which many precious and determining features
had in the classical times of Greece been either
greatly obscured, or even altogether lost.   This re-
mark applies especially, though not exclusively, to
the religion of the nation.

III

The most serious of all the impediments to a
right comprehension of Homer in modern times
has been that the picture of life, manners, and
religion, which he draws, has been viewed through
the discolouring medium of the Latin literature
and mythology.   Through the whole period of
Roman predominance, and during the long slumber
of the Greek language and of all Hellenism in the
West, these were in exclusive possession of the
field.   Nor were they in the slightest degree

displaced, so far as Homer was concerned, at the Renascence. This Latin medium, instead of merely transmitting the light, disintegrated it, and gave a false effect.

IV

Of this overshadowing and darkening influence, exercised through the Latin tongue, it may be worth while to supply a few illustrations.

1. It supplanted not only the genuine Homeric name of Achaians, but the classical appellations of Hellas and Hellenes ; and imposed the designations of Græcia and Græci, which had no early link with the country or the language, except in the single and perfectly insignificant word *Graia*, once mentioned in the text of the *Iliad*.

2. It bridged over the entire interval between ancient and modern history, and disguised the nature of the transition, necessary to be effected in order to reach the prehistoric time of Homer.

3. Such was the influence of the Latin tongue in the Middle Ages that, at the opening of the fourteenth century, Dante was advised to write his immortal Poem in Latin, as being still the language of literature and thought. And, later in that

century, Petrarch founded all his anticipations of
fame upon his Latin works, now in great measure
forgotten.

4. On the revival of printing, the Athenian
Thucydides, prince of historians, was not intro-
duced to the world until about 1480, and was
then presented in a Latin translation. The
princeps edition of his text only appeared in 1502,
from the press of Aldus.

V

More pointedly, the mischief has been due in
a great degree to the paramount rank deservedly
held by Virgil among the Latin poets. This
result was aided by the vast influence of Dante,
who, in electing the great Court-poet for his guide
to the Underworld, thereby pushed forward his
design of presenting the modern Western Empire
as the heir to the Emperors of Rome. Now,
however splendid may be the merits of Virgil on
his own ground, it cannot, I conceive, be doubted
that he wholly reverses the relative positions held
by the two great peoples of the *Iliad:* and that
he very largely hides or vitiates the traditions of
Homer as to characters, manners, and religion.

Next to this grave cause of dislocation and perversion, and perhaps almost as hurtful, has been the belief, so widely accepted in modern times without the trouble of examination, that Homer was an Asiatic Greek,[1] and therefore a person born after the barbarising invasion of the Dorians. He is thus cut off from the heroic period, brought into connection with times and manners long posterior to his own, and subjected to the falsifying interpretations which alone those times and manners provide.

VII

Further, the great Eastward migration of the subdivided Hellenic races, that had been expelled from the Greek Peninsula by the Dorian conquest, opened new and varied channels, through which there were imported among the Hellenes, and uplifted into a commanding position, fresh supplies of Asiatic traditions, from sources with which,

---

[1] I notice with pleasure the work of Thiersch (Halberstadt, 1832), *Ueber das Zeitalter und Vaterland des Homer, oder Beweis dass Homer vor dem Einfall der Heracliden im Peloponnes gelebt habe.*

apparently, the primitive immigrants into Greece had not been placed in contact. These fresh supplies enlarged, coloured, and distorted the older and simpler traditions, of which Homer is the recorder.

VIII

Whatever the cause or causes may be, it has happened, as matter of fact, that speculation about Homer for generations occupied the ground which should rather have been covered by careful examination of his text, and by the results of such examination. There never had been in modern times, until the present century was well advanced, any close, minute, and comprehensive study of the matters contained in the Poems. Moreover, this method of persistent speculation on the origin of the Poems, which has, so to speak, buzzed in the air around them, and given scope for so many ingenious though discordant theories, greatly dulled the edge of all searching perception of the contents.

IX

It can hardly, however, be denied that a certain share in the trial of the question as to the unity

and authority of the Poems belongs to what may
be termed the higher criticism.   By this I under-
stand that careful observation of the qualities,
and the methods, of the Maker or Poet himself,
which has been so largely applied to Shakespeare
in literature, and very generally to the most
distinguished artists in other branches.   And yet
how small a space, in comparison with other
elements, does this vast and varied subject occupy
in the negative or sceptical Homeric literature.

X

By the facts, or contents, of the Poems, most
conveniently set forth in the German word *Realien*,
I understand all particulars drawn from the text,
in its parts or as a whole, which may be illustrative
either of the Poet himself or of what he saw and
sang : of the world and the lands and the time in
which, and of the men among whom he lived, of
the ideas of those men, and their actions, and the
whole equipment of their life.

XI

The student seriously set upon mastering the

contents of the text will, in all likelihood, first be
struck by their enormous mass ; then by their
variety ; and perhaps last, but most of all, by their
consistency. As respects the point last named, it
is noteworthy that, while many writers have shown
to their own satisfaction that the Poems must be
ascribed to a diversity of sources, the monogra-
phists, usually German, in their humbler but per-
haps more useful office, have found them as a rule
consistent, whereas, if they had sprung from a
number of sources, they must have been frequently
divergent ; have treated them as exhibiting a
unity of the designing mind, and of the picture
drawn ; and have themselves essentially contri-
buted, in their several departments, to establish
that unity.

XII

The extraction and arrangement of the contents
of Homer was begun by Everard Feith, whose
volume of moderate size was published in 1743,
under the title, *Antiquitatum Homericarum Libri
IV.* He was followed by Terpstra in 1831 with
his *Antiquitas Homerica.* A more serious but still
very inadequate effort was that of Friedreich, who
published in 1856, and who first adopted the com-

prehensive title of *Realien*. As the commencement
had been German, so the honour of a complete
performance of the task was reserved to Germany.
After years of Homeric study, Dr. Buchholz of
Berlin, whose death we have now to lament,
published the first portion of his extended and
systematic work, *Die Homerische Realien*, in 1871,
and the last in August 1885.

Throughout this important production, the author
has combined in a single text the *Realien* them-
selves and his interpretation of them. It may be
a question whether the value of the work as an aid
to the student might not even be enhanced, if the
facts and the interpretation were to be separately
presented. Be this as it may, it is perhaps not
too much to say that the vast multitude and mass
of particulars now collected out of the Poems, and
thoroughly digested, each of necessity witnessing
in its degree for or against the rest, are likely to
supply a far more conclusive test of the unity of
the works, and of the nearness of the Poet to the
men and things he deals with, as well as of his
aims, than loose speculation, or even testimonies
which do not ascend to the source, or to an age
near it, in date or in associations.

XIII

Without doubt, Homer sang for bread ; but the particulars, both of the *Iliad* and of the *Odyssey*, clearly show us that the men, to and for whom he sang, pre-eminently valued the links which bound them to preceding times.   Witness the institution, dignity, and influence of the Bards ; the prevalence and familiarity of patronymics, which kept freshly alive the idea of lineal descent ; the use of the more vivid imagery of genealogies, such as we find in Homer, to serve the purposes of chronology, in an age anterior to the use of formal record and extended numeration ; the historic purpose assigned to the monuments of departed heroes; the accounts carefully given of the settlement of countries or districts (such as Scheriè, for example, in *Od.* VII.) ; and the abundance of pre-Troic legends in the *Iliad*, sometimes introduced in situations where the actual recital would have been inconvenient or incongruous.   All this testifies to the strength and activity of the historic aim of the Poet.

The external testimonies[1] concerning the Homeric Poems are scanty, superficial, late, and in some cases certainly erroneous. They are so late, indeed, that the earliest of them is dated six centuries after the reputed era of the Dorian Revolution. It is impossible to build upon them any solid, or even any consistent, history of the Poems. They are in themselves of doubtful interpretation ; and they require largely to be pieced together by hypotheses, no one of which has obtained any semblance of general acceptance. One or two of them however are supported by antecedent probability.

XV

It is a question of cardinal and governing importance what is the true method of Homeric study, as between the following alternatives of treating the fundamental questions of unity and authorship. One is to reason upon and from such meagre testimonies as antiquity has left us respecting their origin and formation. One is to break

[1] These testimonies have been summarily noticed by Mure in his *Literature of Ancient Greece*, vol. ii. pp. 181-183 ; and likewise in my own *Homeric Studies* (Oxford, 1858), vol. i. pp. 47-55.

them up into several independent works, on the ground of individual conjecture. And a third is, steadily to mine deeper and deeper into the text by observation and comparison, with the valuable aids which have been supplied by the archæological researches of the last half century. This method of handling the text involves a provisional, but only a provisional, assumption of its unity.

I propose, as the most reasonable and the most fruitful, the last-named of these three methods.

XVI

By the essential unity of the Poems I mean not only that of each Poem in itself, but of the two Poems. True, their forming conjointly one authentic picture of a certain age and country does not of itself absolutely imply the unity of their authorship. The main implication, however, is that which concerns the contents, and which combines the innumerable particulars of human life and history furnished by the Poems into one body of evidence descriptive of a given race at a given time.

But though individuality, or singleness of authorship, be not of necessity implied in the term of unity thus understood, it will, nevertheless, probably be found that any departure from the hypothesis of singleness embarrasses much more than relieves the inquirer. The extreme solution of Bentley, the more moderate but thoroughly unpoetical suggestion of Grote, the modest and more ancient scheme of the *Chorizontes*, or separators of the authorship of the *Iliad* from that of the *Odyssey*, only dismiss minor or imaginary difficulties in order to bring into the field others of a more formidable kind.

Again, it has happened that certain features of one or both Poems, which have been put forward as principal grounds for controverting the unity of authorship, are converted into substantive evidences in favour of that unity, when we have widened our researches by taking into view the fact that Homer was conversant, of course in different degrees, first with an inner sphere or zone of geography, known to him by experience, and secondly, and far less definitely, with an outer sphere or zone, known to him only by report. This outer sphere is not inhabited by people of his own stock. And so it comes about that the meaning of the supposed discrepancies, in mythology or manners, between the *Iliad* and the *Odyssey*, probably is that they deal, except within Greece and in Ithaca itself, with separate races, and with non-Hellenic varieties of religion. If the manner of handling be the same, much diversity of matter is what we should naturally expect a skilled and conscientious artist to present.

XIX

Since the study of Homer commenced its first modern development in the eighteenth century, most important additions have been made to our knowledge by archæological research in points directly related to the Homeric text. This has occurred particularly in Egypt, in Assyria, in Troas, and at Mycenæ. Entirely new views have now been opened of the opportunities which may have been enjoyed by Homer for receiving and for incorporating in his works both actual foreign knowledge and traditions of the past imported from abroad.

XX

Dividing the Homeric literature into two parts, one of them that which reasons about the text, whether from *a priori* argument or from testimony *a posteriori*, the other that which reasons out of the text itself, and speaking first of the latter of these methods, I cannot but observe that there exist works of early date, such as Wood *On the Genius and Writings of Homer*, and such as Müller's *Homerische Verschule*, which deserve respect in reference to their pioneering office, but which, in other respects, have probably been injurious. They do not indeed pass by the contents of the Poems, but they are extremely slight and insufficient in dealing with them, while they have, through early possession of the field, exercised a large influence on the current course of thought and opinion. In respect of their slightness, they stand in marked contrast with the large number of German monographs on particular subjects touched in the Poems, which are usually distinguished by remarkable comprehensiveness and care.

XXI

This examination of the text has now proceeded to so forward a stage, partly through monographs, and partly by means of comprehensive synthesis of the Homeric world and life, that the pervading community and consistency of the contents remains but little open to question. It has therefore become, to say the least, allowable to regard them not only as a whole, but as a historic whole.

XXII

Such acceptance, as is here recommended, of the Poems as a historic whole, does not of itself require us to believe either that the received text is absolutely pure, or that the events purporting to be historical actually happened, or that the personages lived, as it is recited that they lived and happened respectively. All that is absolutely required by it is to admit that the *Iliad* and *Odyssey* exhibit to us a true rendering of life and manners, at a given time and within a given local circumscription. The body of the Poems may conceivably be to a large extent factitious, and yet their soul may be in the highest sense historical, the one being, as it were, a parable of the other.

And it follows *a fortiori* that the idea of *rifacimento*, or linguistic manipulation without corresponding departure from manners, is a question left open indeterminately to the judgments of competent inquirers. It is one for which I do not possess the necessary qualifications.

XXIII.

Nevertheless I cannot but deem it probable that the larger questions involved in the admissions last made will have to be ultimately determined by internal evidence : by the strength, namely, of that web of cohesion and consistency which supplies the *nexus* of the contents, and shows how almost every line is related to some, if not every other line.

XXIV

Again it may happen, as in the case of the negative speculations concerning unity and author-

C

ship, so also in relation to the Troic events, that by resolving them into pure invention, or into figures, such as (for example) the solar theory, we only exchange smaller for greater difficulties, and lose much to gain little. For, if the recitals are of· facts, they are of great facts, with a great meaning, which projects itself into the general history of the world. For it exhibits a principal stage in the formation of a nationality which is, to speak with moderation, one among the greatest in the whole range of human history, and which has exercised a vast shaping force upon the characters of other nationalities, and upon the whole civilisation of modern times.

XXV

On the other hand, there are important liberties, which still remain intact for those who have found themselves constrained by the evidence to believe in the Poems not only as soul-history but as fact-history. For example, they may exercise a free discretion upon the two following classes of cases.

The first, that of incidents which lie outside the range of ordinary human experience, like the Theophanies, and in fact the entire Theurgy of the Poems.

The second, that of matters where the Poet, following the laws of his art, may have idealised the facts and persons with whom he had to deal, so as to bring them up to the standard of the best and most effective representation, for the enhancement of instruction and delight. For example, the most finely elaborated characters, such as those of Achilles, Odysseus, and Helen; or the three decades of years—the preliminary, the principal, and the epilogistic or concluding, which together make up the full cycle of the transactions associated with the fall of Troy.

XXVI

Like the pre-Troic legends of human history in the *Iliad*, so the Archaic and foreign legends of Olympos are introduced with a high art-purpose. The latter throw light on the genius and structure of the religion, the former performing the same office for the nation. To some of these legends no key has yet been found. But in other cases a design is sufficiently discernible. For example, the journey of Zeus and the Olympian Court in the first *Iliad* to the banquet of the Aithiopes, indicates that the knowledge of Homer went beyond the Achaian limits, and that his gods had, in his view, essential points of community with the gods of other races.

XXVII

If, in every case where legends of gods or men are introduced in the speeches of the Poems, we suppose Homer to have intended a representation of fact as to persons, times, and places, the result is absurd.   For instance, when Achilles in the first book is persuading his mother Thetis to prefer the grand petition to Zeus for the satisfaction of the Wrath, he details to her in full an Olympian legend, which he says that he had often heard her recite in his father's halls, and of which, therefore, it could not be necessary for him to acquaint her with all the particulars (*Il.* I. 396-412).   Again, when Glaukos meets Diomed in arms on the battlefield, instead of fighting they interchange speeches running through nearly a hundred lines (VI. 122-211), of which the chief part is a history of the life of Bellerophon, the great Lycian ancestor. This is utterly incongruous as an incident in the

day's battle, but most instructive as explaining
the derivation of an Achaian race from Lycia, and
the high position held by the Lycians in the war.
The explanation of such legends is to be found in
recognising the historic intention of the Poet, who
by a strong use of licence wove into his text long
passages which break his narrative, but which have
their justification in the deep interest that they
possessed for his hearers.   There can be no good
ground for doubting that this was done to forward
the wide historic aim of the Poem, which carried
him far back into the past.

XXVIII

Upon this idea, however, a question may justly
be. put.   If Homer introduces these passages into
the Poem in order to feed the appetite of his
hearers for their national traditions, why are they
found in the speeches and not in the narrative,
which at first sight would appear to be their
proper place?   Here we touch upon a striking
peculiarity of Homer as compared with other
Epic poets.   His narrative is usually short and
simple : his speeches not only incessant, and often

long, but never merely ornamental or reflective, and always so contrived as to advance the action. This is the manner of the drama, to which Homer approaches in a degree unknown elsewhere. The spirit of both the Poems is intensely and vividly dramatic. And these legends, though they might theoretically have found a more appropriate place in the narrative, would, if so placed, have laid a much heavier weight on the elastic movement of the works, especially of the *Iliad*, to which these remarks principally apply. They find a direct illustration in the speech of Glaukos (*Il.* VI.)

XXIX

Even more important than the speech of Glaukos is the great legend put into the mouth of Thetis by Achilles in the first *Iliad.* The immediate purpose of the hero is to prove to his mother her power, and thereby to leave her no room for evading compliance with his request. This he does by showing how Zeus was indebted to her, and was bound to pay the debt on her demand. So we have a description of the convulsion brought about in the religious system of the country by the conflict of the various elements, imported into it by its various races, and not, as yet, thoroughly compounded. And the method of the reconciliation is exhibited by representing Thetis, who herself belonged mythologically to the order of Nature Powers, as the agent whose activity and resource brought the several influences into harmony under the sovereignty of Zeus.

XXX

The question whether the Poems were written, or recited without writing, may be taken, I conceive, as settled in favour of the latter opinion.

The mode in which the *Iliad* mentions, in one or two passages, the use of inscribed signs to convey ideas of itself goes far to prove that the Achaians knew no form of writing available for the transmission of Poems exceeding respectively 15,000 and 12,000 lines.

Particular passages may supply strong arguments against the contrary hypothesis. The Preface to the Catalogue represents it as a great effort ; and so it was for memory, because there is no such *nexus* in reciting a list of places as in a series of connected events or ideas. But if the Poems were written compositions, to frame the Catalogue would require less and not more than the ordinary effort.

It seems probable that the unwise denial of Wolf's introductory contention against the writing of the Poems, by its explosion made a breach in the wall, through which came in a flood of scepticism unsustained by reason concerning the Poems.

XXXI

An opinion has been held, though it has not prevailed to any wide extent, that the diction of the two Poems respectively differs in date, as well as that the diction of both, and especially of the *Odyssey*, savours of a late age. While leaving these questions to students who have special qualifications, I venture to interject a remark on what we term style in the Poems. There is no author of any date who has a more marked style than Homer : there are very few who come near him in this particularity. It is impossible to take five or ten consecutive lines from any part of the Poems (though I admit a certain heaviness, and declension of spirit, in Od. XXIV.) which could possibly be ascribed to any one except Homer; this observation embraces both the Poems. I find it difficult to conceive how this unity and particularity of style could have been maintained in works largely patched, and made up as to their form, by later hands.

XXXII

Notwithstanding that some few pleas may be urged to a contrary effect, the *Iliad* and the *Odyssey* bear conclusive marks of the same parentage. Among them are these: but nothing more than specimens of argument can be here given.

1. The Homeric style of each severs them from all other works.

2. The mythological variations fit in with true ethnical conceptions as to the two geographical zones respectively, and are therefore such as we should have reason to expect from the author of the *Iliad*.

3. That two such master poets should spring from a race insignificant in numbers at the same or nearly the same time, each of them isolated and each consummate, is of the very highest improbability.

4. The supreme, and except by Shakespeare unapproached, faculty of drawing character, is common in the fullest sense to the two Poems.

5. The particular characters, as they appear in each, are in the finest correspondence with one another.

6. The characters of particular gods, hardly less remarkable as portraits than those of the men, present in the two Poems the same radical harmony as the human characters.

7. The coincidences of the class which we term undesigned will be found almost countless, and their collective strength might appear irresistible.

XXXIII

It may be right to supply a few specimens of these coincidences. They might be indefinitely multiplied.

1. The strong family affections of Odysseus are a leading feature of the *Odyssey*. In the *Iliad* he is the only chieftain who mentions his absent son : and he does it with tenderness and exultation (*Il.* II. 260 ; IV. 354).

2. With the high prerogatives assigned to the use of speech in the *Iliad*, may be compared the striking reply of Odysseus (*Od.* VIII. 169-174).

3. In the two spondaic lines of the *Odyssey*

there is the same evident relation of sound to sense as in the three of the *Iliad*.

4. The later mythology gives horses to the sun : but they are alike withheld in both the Poems.

5. The free use of proper names in considerable numbers to describe by their etymology occupation and race, and so to assist in drawing main lines of the plan, is common to both the Poems. See *Il.* XVIII. 39-49 ; and *Od.* IX. 111-117.

6. Compare the appeal of Thetis to Zeus (*Il.* I. 503-516), and her plea of personal disparagement in the event of refusal, with that of Poseidon (*Od.* XIII. 128-138).

7. Apollo in *Il.* XXI. 468, declines fighting with Poseidon, as being his uncle. Athenè, in *Od.* VI. 329, for the same reason will not act openly in Scheriè on behalf of Odysseus.

8. As to delicacy in the exposure of the person, compare *Od.* VI. 218-222, with *Il.* XXII. 75, and conversely with *Il.* II. 262.

9. Thought is used as an emblem of rapid motion in *Od.* VII. 36, and in *Il.* XV. 80-82. That is to say, once, and once only, in each Poem an abstract idea is employed to illustrate corporeal movement.

10. In *Il.* IX. 70, it is signified that a ruler ought to entertain his friends hospitably : and also in *Od.* XI. 184-186.

11. The epithet θεῖος is used in both Poems with a reserve altogether singular. (See Mure, *Literature of Greece*, vol. ii. p. 81.)

12. It is never applied in either Poem to any living person or class, except a king, a herald, a bard, or one of the two protagonists.

13. Poseidon travels freely in both Poems : but when he appears specially in the character of sea-god, both Poems give him Aigai as his dwelling (*Il.* XIII. 10-31 ; *Od.* V. 381).

14. A good repute in public opinion is highly valued, and the want of it keenly felt. See *Il.* IX. 460 (Phoinix), and *Od.* VI. 29, 273 (Nausicaa).

15. A peculiar designating force of the Greek article without other specification is found in both the Poems, *e.g. Il.* I. 11 ; *Od.* III. 299.

16. While Themis has no substantial part or clear impersonation in either Poem, she has peculiar dignity in both. In the *Iliad* she presides at the Olympian feast (XV. 95), and summons the greater Assembly (XX. IV.) In the *Odyssey* she is, with Zeus, the object of the prayer of Telemachos (II. 68).

17. Arès is the paramour of Aphroditè in *Od.* VIII.; and is placed in peculiar sympathy with her in the *Iliad*, when he lends his chariot (V. 347-363), and when he is led off by her after his defeat (XXI. 416).

18. A wife is promised to Hephaistos by Herè in the *Iliad* where the mythology is Hellenic : but in the *Odyssey*, where for the outer zone it is eastern, Aphroditè is his wife.

19. The character of Aphroditè is disparaged by Homer in a manner quite peculiar to himself : and this is common to both the Poems. In the case of the daughters of Pandarus, she is not even goddess of Beauty.

SECTION II

HOMER AS NATION-MAKER

I

ALL through the Poems of Homer, but especially in the *Iliad*, we trace an aim which was before all things national. Everywhere he forms and fosters the national idea, and equips it at all points.

He cuts off the Achaians from everything that could bear the aspect of derivation from a foreign land or race, and all the evidences we can gather on that subject are incidental and undesigned.

He had to launch into the world what we may term the Greek idea.

He records with singular care and consistency, through the medium of his genealogies, all that can be linked to the Achaian families subsisting at the Troic period, but he nowhere refers the nation

to a foreign origin : nor is he careful to deal with
any foreign legend except it be one (such as that
of Bellerophon, and that of the Phaiakes) to which
he can give an Achaian purpose.

It is part of his design to isolate his race, and
this isolation in the historic times was conspicuous
through the familiar distinction between Greeks
and Barbarians.

II

Absorbed in this Greek idea, he gives himself
wholly to it, and seems as though he had no
superlative care either for heaven or earth, near
or far, old or new, except in relation to the
Achaian race, which it was his office alike to
commemorate and to mould.   For other things
he cared only in relation to that race.   Even his
Thearchy was so constructed as above all things
to reflect Achaian ideas, Achaian characters,
Achaian polity.   Uplifting this race, and its ideal
out of the mass of things human, he furnishes it
with its grand point of departure in the history
of the world, on which it has never since ceased
to exercise a powerful influence.

III

As with regard to remote times, so also is it with regard to remote places.   In no single case does the Poet verbally relate or admit that the beloved country, to which in its ductile stage of existence he could hardly yet dare to give a name, was in debt to any outside place or person for its qualities, habits, or institutions.   Only when we have found certain persons and families to have special relations to particular titles and characteristics of art, manners, and religious traditions, and when we have noted as far as possible the respective starting-points of each, do we obtain indications of the manner in which, through successive immigrations, the factors of the composite Greek whole were supplied.

Though Homer does not speak of autochthons, it is easy to see how, out of this exclusiveness of his, the estimate of autochthonism, as it prevailed in later times, might spring.

IV

The Greek nation has at all times been recognised more or less definitely as composite.   But the Poems represent it to us in a period of its composition, nearer by many centuries to the original commencement of the process, than any other record in our possession. We see the course of its genesis still going on; and the several qualities and attributes of the several constituent factors have not yet been detached from their primary associations, or made common property by complete fusion into a single whole.

V

When the historic aim of the Poems has been taken thoroughly into view, we shall look for the signs of that aim in all cases where it is reasonably to be inferred. We find them in the record of two remarkable pre-Troic efforts : one that of the two consecutive wars of Achaians against Thebans, who are called Kadmeians, and thereby specially marked with the note of foreign origin ; the other the voyage of the ship *Argo*, directed against what was traditionally reported as we know from Herodotos to be an Egyptian colony, and thus falling into line with the retaliatory invasion of Egypt by revolted peoples, in which

it has been held that the monuments show the
Achaians to have taken part.

VI

If the aim of the Poems be historic, their
ethnographical features come to be of high
interest, since they indicate the distinctions of
human manners, pursuits, and religion, as in *Od.*
I. 3.

πολλῶν δ' ἀνθρώπων ἴδεν ἄστεα καὶ νόον ἔγνω·

These may be the key which will give us
a real access to the great Homeric problems of
the actual, and also of the Olympian world ; which,
as to ethnical considerations, follows the actual
in the manner of its articulation.   It is needful
therefore to inquire whether there are any
primary lights on the face of the Poems, indica-
tive of racial origins.

VII

The proper names of persons in Homer are
very generally the vehicles of ideas.   They thus
become a ready means for indicating pursuits and
qualities, not only of individuals, but, when taken
in combination, or formed into groups, for races

also. They thus become the basis of ethnological inductions. The most plainly demonstrative instance is found in the assemblage of sixteen personal names of Phaiakes in Scheriè,[1] who offer themselves as competitors in the games. Every one of these names is etymologically maritime, with the single exception of Thoon. This, however, is derived from the adjective *thoos*, which is with Homer a favourite epithet for ships, and signifies the motive power they carry, commonly called by us *way*. By these names the Phaiakes are pointed out to us as a maritime race ; and, when other particulars are taken into view, ground is laid for connecting them with the Phoinikes.

VIII

The great name of Hellas, which reigned supreme in the historic times until the Romans supplanted it for Europe at large by the less appropriate designation of Greece, is found in Homer in various forms—

a. He names the Helloi or Selloi, ὑποφῆται of

[1] *Od.* VIII. 111-116.

Zeus, his organs or interpreters at Dodona (*Il.* XVI. 234).

b. We have the derivative[1] Hellenes (*Il.* II. 684) used as a local but not as a general national name.

c. We have also a national name supplied in the compound Πανέλληνες (*Il.* II. 530) coextensive with Achaioi.

d. The name Hellas itself appears in many passages, but never for the entire country : it may be said to have loosely signified what was afterwards Thessaly.

e. The designation reappears in the name of Kephallenes, meaning in the *Iliad* the soldiers of Odysseus, in the *Odyssey* his subjects.

IX

The ordinary or stock names of the nation

---

[1] The later tradition bore a rude witness to the earlier, in the mythical story that Hellen was the father of three sons, Aiolos, Doros, and Xouthos, and of two grandsons, Ion and Achaios, four of whom became the eponymists of the chief branches of the race. It was only after the great eastward migration that this mythical story could have come into being. Colonel Mure pointed out that the name Hellen was a derivative (*Literature of Greece*, vol. i. p. 39, *n.*), so the story condemns itself.

which fought against Troy are three in number, and they are so named by Thucydides in the following order :—

1. Danaans.
2. Argeians.
3. Achaians.

Each appears to correspond with a distinct phase in the settlement of the Greek Peninsula : and each also to betoken one of the three great factors of the Hellenic stock.

X

The Achaian name is used, in the masculine gender, with a few cases of the feminine, nearly 800 times, to designate the people : the Argeian 188 times : the Danaan 147.

The first is represented in the territorial name Achaiis, the second in Argos ; and both these terms appear to have been familiar. The third is according to all indications the senior of the three appellatives, but is not represented in any territorial name, as though it had had less to do, in bulk, with peopling the country, and had thus a slighter hold upon the national tradition.

XI

In following carefully the uses of these several appellatives, it will be found that the Achaian name has a decided leaning to the aristocratic and historically most distinguished portion of the community. The Argeian name leans to the masses. The Danaan is an archaic name, which perhaps had never been in actual use for the whole people, and in the Poems it has a specially military colour. These uses are illustrated by the text of the *Odyssey*, where the Danaan name altogether disappears, except in connection with a recital of the war. In this Poem the use of the names is less frequent, but the distinctions between them are maintained.

XII

In one passage only of the Poems do we find any two of the three names in combination as adjective and substantive. The line (*Od.* VIII. 538) is as follows—

'Αργείων Δαναῶν ἠδ' 'Ιλίου οἶτον ἀκούων·

It occurs in a description of Odysseus listening to a Trojan lay, which was sung in the palace of

Alkinoos. Are we in this place to understand
the Argeian Danaans, or the Danaan Argeians?
For I take it as certain that the two words refer
to the same subjects. The Danaan name is used
twelve times in the *Odyssey*, the Argeian (apart
from Helen) seventeen. No light is supplied by
these facts. The Danaan name is associated with
Greece only in the North-Eastern Peloponnesos
and long before the war, at the time of contact
with and probable subjection to Egypt, and her
maritime agents the Phœnicians. Now if Danaan
were a Phœnician name, and the Phaiakes were,
as appears most probable, of Phœnician line and
association, then it seems most appropriate to
include in the description of the army before
Troy terms of a Phœnician colour; while avoid-
ing confusion by the turn of the phrase, calling
them those Danaans who were connected with
the Argeian name and country, the Argeian
Danaans.

XIII

The name Argos in Homer is one of great
significance. It is used on special occasions, in
Il. II. 559, and VI. 52, for the capital of a section

of the country ; but it is also used to designate
the whole country which supplied the army before
Troy.   Again it is employed in III. 75 and 258,
jointly with Achaiis, to designate the entire
country.   We have some guidance towards the
distribution of the territory between the two
appellatives in the phrase *Argos Achaiichon, Il.* IX.
141, 283.   This phrase appears probably to mean
the Argos which was the centre of Achaian power,
namely the Peloponnese.   Comparing with these
passages the line II. 681, we find Thessaly as
a whole to have been designated the *Argos
Pelasgicon ;* and the Zeus of Dodona was (XVI.
233) Pelasgic Zeus.   Thus the word Argos in its
larger sense runs over the entire country, and it is
in conformity herewith that the name of Argeioi
is applied to the army at large ; while, on the other
hand, the characteristic epithet *Argeie* so often
applied to Helen meant Helen of Argos in the
narrower sense of the specially Agamemnonian
dominion.

XIV

While the names of Argeioi and Danaoi both
disappear from use in the *Odyssey*, excepting in a

retrospective manner, they differ in this respect
that Argeioi has, and Danaoi has not, a leaning
towards the mass of the people. Were we to
exchange the indeterminate for the determinate,
we might say that *Danaoi* means properly the
soldiers, *Argeioi* the people, *Achaioi* the chiefs.

XV

In support of the special signification which I
attach to the word *Argeioi*, the following observa-
tions may be adduced :—

a. Its disappearance (except retrospectively)
from the *Odyssey* is in close accordance
with the fact that in that Poem the Pen-
insula and people are never dealt with as
a whole, but we have particular persons
or districts only brought before us.

b. It is a territorial rather than a race-name,
and it stands alone in its embracing the
entire territory.

c. It is never used when the chiefs are spoken of
distinctively or apart from the army.

d. It may be conjectured to mean field-workers :

as *argon*[1] is an old form of *ergon*, and *ergon* without specialising epithet signifies principally (in the plural) operations of agriculture.

XVI

Achaiis is also used as a territorial name, both adjectively with *gaia* (*Il.* I. 254 ; VII. 124) and substantively (III. 75, 258 ; XI. 769). In two of these passages it is used alone, and evidently covers the whole country. In XI. 770 it may have the same signification, or may (less probably) be limited to the country to which Achilles and the Hellic people were specially related. In the two passages from the Third Book we have the words, " To horse-feeding Argos, and Achaiis, fair women's land." It is not likely that the Poet would give the epithet fair women's land (Kalligunaika) to one portion of the country : and probably the word here means the whole, while Argos is named as the royal and metropolitan province. The Peloponnese is however the Achaic Argos as distinguished from Thessaly the Pelasgian. All Greece was Achaiis, and the inhabitants of its

---

[1] *Juventus Mundi*, p. 54.

sections were either everywhere or to a large extent called Achaioi, as we may see from *Il.* II. 562, 684, and *Od.* XXIV. 438.

XVII

The proof of my proposition that the Achaian name in the Poems, though frequently applied to the army or nation at large, has a leaning to the chiefs and aristocracy, depends upon a large number of passages. I will take one as, for the *Iliad, instar omnium.* In the Teichoscopy, when the armies are gathered in the field, Priam, on the walls, asks Helen for information respecting the persons of different chiefs who are present with their several contingents. First comes Agamemnon, and the question put is, "Who is this Achaian warrior?" (III. 167). Then comes Odysseus, with another identifying mark. Thirdly, the King points to Aias (or Ajax), and again employs the epithet Achaian as a distinctive word. But he fixes it further by saying, "Who is this other Achaian warrior who stands, taller by head and shoulders, among the Argeians?" (III. 226), evidently meaning the soldiery around him.

XVIII

This great name of Achaians overshadows every other.   In the course of the *Iliad* alone it is used I think, in one or other of its grammatical forms, over 640 times, and more than twice as often as all the other appellatives put together.   It is in fact the true contemporary national name of the people that conquered Troy ; and the undeniable though partial civilisation of that people, the first grand manifestation of Hellenism is, and as I conceive ought to be called, the Achaian civilisation. They may from use be called Greeks, but it is only in a secondary and improper sense.   And that secondary sense becomes a very misleading one, if it be allowed to draw off our minds from the fact that this Achaian civilisation is independent and historical, and is somewhat broadly distinguished, sometimes to its great advantage, from the later and more splendid civilisation of Greece.

XIX

We are therefore justified in looking, and indeed required, as searchers, to look at the meanings of names, whether individual or national, so as not to use them only for the purpose of designation, whenever those meanings can be found, and are illustrative of matters relevant to the purpose of the Poems. This rule will be found to run very far, and to open up some really important parts of the sense which the Poet means to convey.

XX

Homer gives the name of Phoinikes to the remarkable maritime people on whom the Greek Peninsula was dependent for all that came to it over sea ; not only in articles of trade, but in knowledge of the arts of life. Their maritime traffic embraced Egypt and Libya as well as the Syrian coast, to say nothing now of the regions westward, so that the name is related in Homer to everything which arrived, and everything which was learned, by ship from the south and south-east. And, in order to embrace this great aggregate in a collective appellation, I call by the name of Phœnicianism everything within the Greek limits that savours of derivation from those quarters.

XXI

So far as the text of Homer carries us, we find marked notes of Phœnicianism in the following portions of the Peninsula.

1. Bœotia, from the (Egyptian) names of Thebai and Hupothebai: the worship of Poseidon at Ongchestos (*Il.* II. 506), which was not a port: the Achaian wars, which are described as against not fellow-Achaians but Kadmeians: and the traditions of Antiopè (*Od.* XI. 260-265) and Epicastè (*Ibid.* 271-280).

2. The nook of Sikuon, from the legend of Sisuphos in *Il.* VI., and from indications in the *Odyssey*.

3. The Western Peloponnese, from the legend of Turo (*Od.* XI. 235-259), and the position of Nestor with his descent, and his Poseidon-worship, in *Od.* III.

4. The North-Eastern Peloponnese, from the pre-Troic legends of which it is the seat.

5. Ithaca, from a combination of very diversified features, requiring to be considered in their aggregate.

The legend of Glaukos in *Il.* VI., which with-
draws that noble chieftain from an impending
conflict with Diomed, in the first place illustrates
the uniform care of the Poet to do honour to the
Lycian name. Secondly, he gives to Glaukos a
Phœnician lineage. For there are no more absol-
ute marks of Phœnicianism than the use of the
names Ephurè and Aiolid (*Il.* VI. 152-154).
Thirdly, he places this ancestor of the Lycian
chieftain upon the Gulf of Corinth. And fourthly,
he declares that there was a hereditary xeinian
bond, or bond of hospitality, between Glaukos
and a prime Achaian prince and warrior. This
example may serve as an indication of the place
assigned to the Phœnician element, as one of the
grand factors, by settlement in the Peninsula, of
the Achaian nation. It also betrays to us the
reason of the marked and otherwise inexplicable
predilection which the Poet shows for the Lycians
among the Trojan *epicouroi* or allies, namely their
kinship with Greece.

XXIII

The prayer of *Il.* XVI. (233-249), offered by
Achilles to Zeus, is the most remarkable of the
many prayers in the Poem.   In the fate of Patro-
clos, it deals with the central hinge of the Trojan
war.   In its theology it is purely monotheistic ;
and it treats Zeus as the sole arbiter.   What we
have here specially to note is the importance of
this prayer in relation to the Achaian nationality.
First Achilles, who offers it, is not only the
protagonist of the Poem, constructed on a colossal
and almost preter-human scale, but is also, among
all the warriors, the one most properly Achaian
and Hellenic : and indeed both these names are
assigned, with an evident significance, to his
contingent alone (*Il.* II. 684).   He is the truly
national hero in a sense quite distinct from that
of the political headship, which Homer, possibly,
or probably in deference to actual history, has
allotted to Agamemnon.   Likewise Zeus is the
truly national god.   Accordingly, he is described
as Pelasgic, and as Dodonian ; and this last epithet
appears to be illustrated by the introduction of the
Helloi, his ministers and votaries, and the source of

the Hellenic stock. Thus he is associated with two great race-factors of the Achaian nation. For the third or Phœnician factor, however important, was, except in Bœotia, not racial, but existed only in dominant families.

XXIV

In this great cardinal prayer there are other points not unworthy of notice. It consecrates, as it were, by a solemn religious Proem, the new departure in the conduct of Achilles, which, from the moment of sending forth Patroclos, on an errand perfectly justified by his computation of relative martial superiority, is consecutive and unchanging throughout. Again it is distinguished, among the Homeric prayers, by its length, and particularity, and by the formality of its Invocation, which, in this case alone, includes a recital concerning the worshippers of the Deity invoked. And further, it is placed on a higher level than that of the other Homeric prayers, by being more strictly intercessory ; it is the prayer of an individual for another individual.

It is in effect the foundation stone of the whole subsequent action of the Poem.

E

XXV

The connection of Achilles with Homeric nationalism is further exhibited in the following among other ways :—

1. On the Thearchic side of the Poem he is associated, through his mother Thetis, silver-footed daughter of Nereus, with the old Nature-cult of the country ; while by his father he is descended, in the Aiakid line, from Zeus, now set forth as in the fullest sense the Achaian Zeus.

2. Although the numerical force of his contingent was secondary (fifty ships, II. 685), yet the usual order of the Catalogue is varied, so as to introduce it with a Proem which marks off the whole Pelasgic Argos, or Thessaly, as the region which, if not subject throughout to the sovereignty of his house, yet is assigned to him in this sense, that it is not allowed to contribute any other prominent or important figure to the action of the Poem.   Although in the aggregate this region supplies no less than two hundred and eighty ships, the whole stage is kept clear for the one dominant character.

3. The phrase Pelasgic Argos (II. 681) appears

to show at least the numerical preponderance of
the senior race in this region. But the subjects of
Achilles are denominated specially in *Il.* II. 684
as Achaians ; and the whole region seems in *Il.*
III. 75, 258, to be denoted as the Achaiis of the
Poems : a phrase for which it seems difficult to
assign a reason except its having produced Achilles.

XXVI

Except as to the Kadmeians, who have no
special significance in the war, the Phoinikes no-
where appear in Greece as a people, colony, or
race. They are only traceable in the thread-
lines of particular families. Their importance can
hardly be overrated : but they must be weighed,
not counted. It has been supposed by some that
the Homeric Greeks were Aiolians. The (mythical)
genealogy, which makes Hellen the parent of the
nation, gives him Aiolos for his eldest son. The
kernel of truth in this myth is that Aiolids (never
called in Homer Aiolians) may be traced, by their
longer genealogies, to an older standing in Greece
than Achaians, who were already famous at the
Troic period ; and they are older in fame than
Dorians or Ionians, though these two are both found

locally in the Poems.   The two most palpable
notes of Phœnician lineage are (1) connection
with the name of Aiolos (*Il.* VI. 154 ; *Od.* XI.
236) and (2) descent from Poseidon.

XXVII

The Phoinikes of Homer may be described
roughly in one word as merchant-pirates : traders,
kidnappers, and buccaneers.   The immigrant Phœ-
nician element has a wider meaning.   As between
the two, they were upon the whole a great intellectual
force ; a deteriorating moral element.   With them
is associated almost every rudiment of art and
manners which we find mentioned in the Poems.
For example : the art of navigation ; of stone-build-
ing ; of work in metals, with a close approach to Fine
Art ; of embroidery ; of medicine, and a chemistry
however simple ; the institution of the Games ; the
importation of the horse, and the art, nay arts, of
horse-driving (*Il.* XXIII. 402-447, 566-601). Pos-
sibly even the driving of the plough in a superior
manner.   Not that these belonged to Phœnician
sailors ; but they belonged to the countries of
Phœnician traffic and to immigrants brought by
their ships.   We also trace the foreigner, and

this variously, in the manufacture of arms. But the policy of the Phoinikes proper was to avoid intervention in quarrels not their own.

XXVIII

It seems probable that we are to consider the gift of song as an exception. For this gift of song has been markedly assigned to Achilles, and to him alone (*Il.* IX. 186-189). It is almost the only gift which is not ascribed to the all-accomplished Odysseus, who is even a consummate ploughman and mower, as well as artificer (*Od.* XVIII. 365-375). The two protagonists are evidently the two greatest orators of the Poems. In Homer the two elements materially or numerically strongest are the Hellenic and the Pelasgian. The two elements, between which the higher gifts and properties are divided, are; the Hellenic and the Phœnician. The Phœnician share was in progress made, in accomplishments possessed. The Hellenic share lay in the region higher still : in character, in purpose, in force of will, in creative genius : in the many-sided capability of assimilating, and of reproducing, multiplied thirty, sixty, and a hundred fold, the importations from the East.

XXIX

What then, it may be asked, has the Poet reserved for the third factor in the composition of the nation, for his Pelasgian people? Of the loftier endowments little. It is observable (*a*) that they are named among the populations of Crete (*Od.* XIX. 177); (*b*) that they are never mentioned by Homer, even as serving in the Trojan army, without a favourable epithet; (*c*) that the etymology of the names among the common soldiery points to them as engaged in the pursuits of rural life, and sometimes as accumulators of substance. We may credit them with the gifts of soldiery, industry, and order. In point of higher qualities they were undeveloped. Perhaps they may be called a nation in the gristle.

XXX

It would be generally allowed that the first commanding factor in the compound, that of Hellenic or Achaian character, is represented in the great and towering personality of Achilles.

After long consideration and inquiry I have arrived at an opinion that the second or Phœnician element, of course in its amalgamation with the paramount stock, is set before us in the character and the position of Odysseus. His character, besides universality of accomplishment, exhibits to us, in their highest development, activity, persistency, comprehensiveness, and design leaning towards craft. As to his position, I have endeavoured to show in another connection [1] how it will be found on examination that the small Ithacan kingdom abounds in signs of Phœnicianism.

XXXI

If the final judgment of Homerologists shall affirm these general conclusions with regard to the composition of the great Hellenic race, and more specifically the propositions last stated, we shall have in them a most interesting view of the completeness and symmetry of the Poet's mind in his dealing with the several factors of the compound nationality, and in the provision made for their personal presentation to his hearers in the characters of his two protagonists.

[1] *Nineteenth Century* for August 1889.

SECTION III

HOMER AS RELIGION-MAKER

I

IF Homer lived and sung as a great creative genius, at a period when his nation was in course of formation ; and if, with whatever degree of consciousness, he exercised his art so as to promote that formation, it was in the nature of the case hardly possible that he should not contribute largely to the formation of a national unity in religion, for without this there could in those days be no national unity at all. The nation, as we have seen, was composite. Apart from the question of a Divine revelation, which is not here supposed, the peoples of antiquity, each according to its several genius, developed great differences in their particular forms of religion. Their systems stood on the same footing as to authority, and when brought locally together, their divergence and the chance of possible conflict required that they should be moulded into some kind of concord. A composite nation, with a strong national spirit, required to arrive at a composite religion.

II

The necessity for a *formula concordiæ*, or, in modern phrase, a *modus vivendi*, was raised to the highest point in a case like that of the Greek Peninsula, where, before the dominant political factors found their way into the country, a local worship, which appears to have been a *cultus* of the Nature-Powers, was evidently in possession of the ground. The Phœnician and Achaian elements respectively were associated with power, as invaders, or as immigrants of high station and authority; so that power stood on one side, numbers and possession on the other. But neither were these powerful influences in accord with one another; both the local sources and the moral standard being materially different.

III

The diversity of the religious traditions con-
stituted the greatest obstacle to the attainment of
the high national aim ; because for each of the
branches these traditions demanded recognition
and manifestation in the common outward acts of
religion, elicited by the ever-returning occasions of
daily life. Thus was continually raised the question
which traditions should prevail, and whether their
relations to one another should be in harmony or
in conflict. And so, conversely, the reciprocal
relations of the religious acts raised also the
question what should be the reciprocal relations
of the persons performing them.

IV

It is then plain that, if the function of Homer
as nation - maker had for its main object to
combine in one harmonious polity the men of the
three great descents—Pelasgian, Phœnician, and
Achaian,—that function must also touch the
question of their several religions, and must be
helped by establishing an unity among them. The

nature and limits of that unity we shall have hereafter to specify, that we may not exaggerate the office of a poet so great and having such an access to the minds of his countrymen through the medium of their institutions.

V

We thus appear to obtain, from a consideration of the natural course of facts, an insight into the *rationale* of those peculiar local traditions in Greece which tell of contests between different deities for different points of the territory, and of the issue of those contests ; they cannot do otherwise than signify the original conflict or competition of religious traditions between the respective sectaries of the older and newer populations, and their settling down into an unity. It is thus, for example, that we may discern in the Twenty-First *Odyssey* the accommodation between the Sun-god · Apollo brought from the East, and perhaps there supreme, and the far loftier conception of the obedient son Apollo such as he stands in the Olympian system.

VI

Of these traditions, outside Homer, some related to Corinth and its neighbourhood. Here it is that Poseidon struggles for the supremacy of the region against Helios, and obtains the coasting district, where the descendant of Aiolos, an Eastern personage, had settled. The upper tract is afterwards made over by Helios to Aphroditè. The first of these two may well be related to a pre-Homeric state of the facts, when the Poseidon worship, imported several generations before the Trojan war, might come into competition with an old Sun worship of the Pelasgian population generally prevailing. The second is as clearly post-Homeric ; for, at the period of the Poems, the Aphroditè worship, though it has passed from Cyprus to Cythera, has not yet obtained a footing on the mainland of Greece. So that it would be out of place, as would probably be a Poseidon worship in Attica or Athens.

VII

We find many indications of the difficulties, which beset the path of the Poet in the execution of his compounding office. One who dwells like Plato in the region of abstract ideas may find fault with him for admitting within his thearchy elements of too low a standard. But he was one who had to deal with the facts of his race and his time ; and the careful investigator of the Poems will find cause for wonder as well as satisfaction at the persistency with which he has excluded from his system the most degrading ingredients in which the religions around him abounded ; the pollution of our nature by the lust-worship of the East, and the disparagement done to it by the *cultus* of the lower animals, and of material objects exhibited in the great Nature-forces. He seems only to have tolerated persons and ideas belonging to the foreign systems as long and as far as he could work them into some kind of consistency with the national genius, and with his Olympian ideal.

VIII

Not only is the Homeric Thearchy composite as a whole, but each divinity is often composite within itself, and comprehends elements derived from more than one of the three great sources of the Poet's theology. Thus the Artemis, who is whipped by Herè in the Theomachy, is the gross figure of Asiatic worship with a hundred breasts, and not the pure and beautiful Artemis who administers the law of painless death, and is besought by Penelope to deliver her from her troubles (*Od.* XVIII. 201). And the Apollo, who appears as a jester in the foreign episode of Arès and Aphroditè, is very different from the Apollo who throughout the *Iliad* is the right arm of Providence, and who in the *Odyssey* mysteriously presides over the trial of the bow.

IX

The Olympian gods of the *Iliad* are divided into an Achaian and a Trojan party. The censure of Plato on Homer for dealing lightly with the deities is really much more applicable to the religion of his own time, as it is exhibited in Aristophanes. No deity of the Hellenic party is ever disparaged by Homer ; and upon what principle was he bound to pay great respect to foreign deities as such, when they were in conflict with

Achaian nationality and with substantial justice? Arès and the Asiatic Artemis are the deities seriously disparaged in the Theomachy; Aphroditè everywhere and with great justice.

X

The religion of Troy, as exhibited in the *Iliad*, differs materially from that of the Achaians, in that it is largely based on the worship of the Nature-Powers. This is conclusively shown from *Il.* III. 103, 104, where it is arranged that the Trojans are to offer lambs to Earth and the Sun, while the Achaians are to offer a lamb to Zeus. Hence again Helios, though as a Nature-Power he is not admitted into Olympos, nor allowed to take any part in the Theomachy, yet is a partisan of Troy, and puts an end with reluctance to the day which was to witness the last of the Trojan successes (*Il.* XVIII.) And hence again Scamandros, the only Nature-Power in the Theomachy, contends on the Trojan side, and is indeed its best supporter. It may be for the same reason that the Nature-Powers generally are summoned to the Great Assembly on Olympos, which authorises the divinities of each party to assist their friends.

XI

Homer has carefully severed his Apollo from the character of a Nature-Power, by investing the Sun with a separate personality. He appears indeed in the Theomachy on the Trojan side, and his mother Leto is there also, probably as an appendage to him. But this arrangement has reference to the fact that he is always the organ of the will of Zeus : and that the plot of the Poem, which required the sin of Agamemnon to be rebuked by the temporary success of his foes, allowed the will and action of Zeus to take the Trojan side until that purpose had been accomplished.

XII

The disposition to incorporate deity with humanity, which I venture to term the theanthropic [1] spirit, and which, though belonging properly to the Hellenic sphere, pervades the whole of the Poems, finds its most marked exhibition in

[1] The phrase anthropomorphism, which has obtained much currency, is open to the objection that it is not wide enough for the case ; since the term *morphè* may be said to be exclusively applicable to material form.

the characters of those higher gods who inhabit Olympos. These, except as to dimension both physical and mental, are cast in the human mould ; subject however to these two conditions, of which the one tends to exalt, and the other to lower them.

1. That when they are dealing collectively with the business of governing the world, they give signs of a certain gravity, sense of duty, and consciousness of moral responsibility for the use of their power over men.

2. That in many of them individually, as in most men of all times, increased capacity principally exhibits itself in increased indulgence.

It is also needful to bear in mind that these deities fall into classes, differing widely one from the other.

And that a portion of what has been let slip from the full Divine idea has been as it were saved and reproduced in the majestic conception of the Eriniies, as well as in the dark and powerful, but ethically less exalted, *Moira* or Fate.

. XIII

The differences between the divinities are not exclusively those of rank, local origin, or ethno-

F

logical connection ; they also rest upon broad
grounds, both intellectual and moral.   There is little
in common as to essence between the conception
of the debased Aphroditè, and the lofty imperson-
ation of Athenè as absolute in intellect and in
power.   And there is no more between the brutal
Arès and the Apollo who, in the whole action of the
Iliad, both conforms and gives effect to the will of
Zeus.   Still, I think it has to be allowed that the
moral element is less emphatically represented in
the individual action of the gods than it is among
men.   There is no god of the Poems (unless it be
the purely abstracted *theos*, who is constantly in
the background of the scene) that is so *good* as
the swineherd Eumaios.

XIV

The collective action of the Olympian gods,
who are the *classe dirigeante* of Homeric antiquity,
is higher not only than their individual, but than
their collective character.   In the main, it befriends
righteousness and the righteous man, and is adverse
to the unrighteous and to wrong at large.   There
is an habitual ascription of righteousness in the

Poems to *theos* and to the *theoi*, which, if not absolutely free from caprice or other imperfection, yet as a general rule completely makes good for them the standard of character and action which has just been described. In this conception there is no alliance with meanness, impurity, or weakness. Nor are *theos* and *theoi* merely abstract ideas ; they are true personalities, but cleansed by severance from what is eccentric or depraved among the actual gods of Olympos.

XV

It is possible to carry up to a certain point the principle of discrimination among the prominent or Olympian deities according to local origin, or racial affinities and sympathies which are connected with it.

a. We may rank as imported from the south and south-east, and as specially associated with the Phœnician name.

1. Poseidon.   3. Aphroditè.
2. Hermes.   4. Hephaistos.
5. Dionusos.

b. There are residuary Nature-Powers, no longer

invested with actual function in the govern-
ment of the world so far as the Achaian
race are concerned.   ˙

1. Aidoneus.   3. Demeter.
2. Helios.   4. Gaia.

c. We have also deities in whose equipment
we find the marks of foreign or inferior
traditions, but whom Homer has effectually
transfigured for the purposes of his thean-
thropic religion.

1. Herè.
2. Artemis. .

d. And we have such as embody, if with varying
admixtures, much loftier conceptions with
reference to the supremacy of Deity, its
illuminating intelligence, and even its re-
deeming action, than can be accounted
for by mere reference to the before-named
sources.   These are—

1. Zeus.
2. Athenè.
3. Apollo.
4. Leto.

XVI

First in the active Olympian Thearchy, as given by Homer, come the five greater gods, not so defined, but so exhibited in action and character. These are—

    1. Zeus.   3. Herè.
    2. Poseidon.   4. Athenè.
             5. Apollo.

But of these Poseidon is wholly exotic, and Herè is, in all that is central to her, indigenous, Achaian, national.

XVII

In each of these five greatest among the Olympian gods, as they are exhibited in the Poems, we find a dominant or characteristic idea.

In Zeus it is policy, a care not confined to Greece.

In Herè it is the Achaian nationality.

In Poseidon it is physical might, with a singular absence of moral elements.

In Athenè it is intellect, supreme in the uniform attainment of its end.

In Apollo it is obedience to Zeus, not by effort, but from pure conformity of will.

XVIII

There are other personages whom we find present in Olympos, though without important functions of government over men.   Such are—

1. Themis, who has a high precedence, and a supreme messengership.

2. Iris, the messenger in ordinary, a conception of extraordinary beauty.

3. Hebè, the cup-bearer.

4. Paieon, the physician.

5. Dionè, mother of Aphroditè, without function. Nor is it possible to omit Persephonè, whose place is in the Underworld.   She is thus severed from Olympos, but appears alone in the actual exercise of power below.

In the eighteenth *Iliad*, Hephaistos has fabricated twenty seats which moved automatically for the Olympian gods.   This number may, as appears probable, have been suggested by the Assyrian tradition.   It may have been conceived rather vaguely by Homer.   The number of deities enumerated above amounts in all to twenty-one.   The titles of Gaia and Persephonè appear, on grounds belonging to each, to be doubtful.

XIX

There is, besides the ordinary assembly or council (*Boulè*) of the gods, a greater Olympian assembly, corresponding with the Agorè or mass-meeting of the Greek community. It includes (*Il.* XX. 4-10) the Nature-Powers at large, with the single and marked exception of Okeanos. He is probably exempted on account of the dignity attaching to him as the great Origin, which stands in contrast with the rather negative place assigned to the Nature-Powers on this occasion. Their presence seems to give validity to the sentence under which the Theomachy takes place ; but it is a presence, and nothing more ; there is not, as in the case of the human assembly, any decision or assent actually recorded.

XX

The population of Homer's preter-human world is multifarious, and not altogether easy to classify. I present it, however, as follows—

1. Olympian gods, ordinary or proper.

2. Retired or deposed dynasties: Okeanos in the first category, Kronos in the second.

3. Nature-Powers, having no share in the government of the Achaian world, such as the Sun (Helios) and the Earth (Gaia).

4. Purely figurative personages, such as *Ossa, Phuza, Kudoimos*, and the like.

5. Impersonated ideas of moral or super-sensible objects, such as the Erinües, Moira, and Sleep with his brother Death (*Hupnos, Thanatos*).

6. The alien and condemned Powers, namely the Titans and the Giants.

7. The minor and purely local Nature-Powers —that is to say, personalities given to Rivers, Fountains, Mountains, Trees.

8. Deified mortals, beginning to find their way into some kind of beatification: Heracles in Olympos, Ino in the sea or sky.

9. The spirits of the dead.

XXI

In Zeus we have a remarkable assemblage of characters not always the most homogeneous.

1. He is the head of the Olympian Court and Polity.

2. In union with that court he is the chief

Executive Governor of human affairs within the limits of the Achaian Peninsula, and of Troas as associated with Achaian action.

3. He is the chief national god both of the old Pelasgian and the new Achaian or Hellenic stock. A struggle for the maintenance of his supremacy, or for the amalgamation of the competing worships is indicated in the curious legend of *Il.* I. 396-406.

4. As towards men, he is the exclusive source of the political authority of sovereigns.

5. He is what may be called the residuary legatee of the old monotheism. In this character his supremacy passes beyond the Hellenic circle into the zone of the outer geography, where the execution is in the hands of other divinities ; and it is thus also that he directs his gaze in *Il.* XIII. 3-6 over the nations northward of the Balkan mountains. To him accrue the care of the poor and the suppliant. He is exempt from all particular enmities. In the government of man he is moderate and passionless, and acts as peacemaker in the Ithacan civil war (*Od.* XXIV. 539-548).

6. He is the person in whom, under the action of the theanthropic idea, human qualities and

passions are most broadly and universally developed, both for good and for evil : affection on the one side, cynical selfishness and lust on the other, with a great dislike to be disturbed or bored.

XXII

The Olympian, like the Achaian, system is governed mainly by opinion. Its head views the fall of Troy with an evident reluctance. The fatal sentence is really carried by the united action of the three deities who after Zeus are the most powerful, namely Poseidon, Herè, and Athenè; Apollo being put out of the case, as he has no decided volition apart from that of Zeus. Troy, on the other hand, is only supported by Divinities of a feebler mould. To secure the rescue of Hector's body (*Il.* XXIV. 65), and even to disarm the single-handed hostility of Poseidon in the *Odyssey*—that is to say, in its Outer zone—Zeus has recourse to the authority of the Olympian assembly (*Od.* I. 77-79). He is apt to look for expedients of accommodation, as when Helios has taken what, under the principles of the system, is reasonable offence (*Od.* XII. 374-388). He threatens largely the use of his reserved stock of force (*Il.* I. 566 *et alibi*), but does not employ it against the three above named, though he is ready to do it against Poseidon singly (*Il.* XV. 176-183), or against Herè with Athenè (*Il.* VIII. 399, 403). Both these however touch cases of offence against a collective decision of the gods.

XXIII

Theanthropy, as an intimate combination of the divine and human natures, is the principle on which Homer has elaborately constructed his Olympian system, and the after history of his country bears testimony to the care, solidity, and comprehensiveness of his work, which was doubtless founded in a clear and keen appreciation of the genius and the mental wants of his countrymen. This principle was in due time exhibited as the basis of Greek life, in religion, in history, and beyond all in Art. It is an idea eminently original; for what has been called anthropomorphism in other schemes bears only the faintest and rudest resemblance to the subtle and refined conception wrought out by Homer, with a care only equalled by that which he has bestowed on the twin conception of nationality.   In all this we see the vigour of his revulsion from the mere nature cult, and the Egyptian and Eastern worships.

XXIV

The religion of Egypt in so far approached the Olympian system, that it freely exhibited deity in created forms.   But it utterly violated the Greek ideal by placing brute and human natures on a level, and using the two combinedly for the representation of the Divine.   It even did this in the most repulsive manner, by assigning the head, or imperial part of the frame, to beast or bird, and leaving the inferior function to humanity in the trunk and members.   So we have the human figure with the cow head, and with the hawk head. Symbolism of this kind, it now seems certain, may have been before the eyes of the Poet and his contemporaries.   He perhaps could not afford wholly to break with it in his impersonations. Accordingly, he assigns to Herè the eye proper to kine, and consecrates the hawk to Apollo.

XXV

Much more largely, in all likelihood, must he have had before him the institutions and emblems of the nature cult. Of these it may be said that sun, moon, and stars, visible and in definite form, did not need the intervention of statuary to interpret them ; and that such substitution could not, as a rule, have prevailed in the Achaian age as an indigenous practice, by reason of the backwardness of art. And it may be doubted whether, if they had been represented in visible images, it would have been possible for him to throw these Nature-Powers so completely into the background of his Poems ; especially the moon, who had so high a place in Assyria, who was worshipped in later times as one of the forms of Diana, and who in Homer is not only not a deity but not even a person. It is probable that the Poet found it the more necessary to disarm as it were certain deities, in cases where they had a high place in foreign or in ancient associations, as these were the most likely to interfere with his great theanthropic design, which united heaven and earth. It is the more remarkable in the case of Selenè from the fact that she resumed her personality in the Pseudo-Homeric Hymns, through the title *anassa*, and the epithets *leukolenos* and *euplokamos*.

XXVI

That he did thus thrust them out of view appears undeniable, and this not only with regard to celestial bodies. From his high place as a member of the Triad, Aidoneus must have been at some time and place a great, perhaps a supreme divinity ; but while he is relegated to the Under-world, he is never named in prayers relating to it, and there is but little sign of his performing any function there. But this method of relegation was practised by him in a manner which is even start-ling. It even seems as though he meant to make it the ordinary abode of the Nature-Powers. This appears from the Address of Achilles, in *Il.* XXIII. 144, to the Shade of Patroclos, in which he intrusts his friend, now on his way to Hades, with a message for the River-God Spercheios.

XXVII

Further indications of this remarkable anta-gonism to nature worship are found, *inter alia :—*

1. In its marking off the religion of Troas from that of Greece.

2. In the repression of Demeter who, though she had been, like Leto, a consort of Zeus, is no more than a lay figure in the Poems.

3. In his never confounding Zeus with atmosphere, or Poseidon with water, and in the broad severance of Nereus who dwells in the hollows of the sea, and is only named indirectly.

4. In his similarly severing Hephaistos from fire, except in one instance where the old or alien usage as it were peeps into the Poems (*Il.* II. 426).[1]

5. From his changing the symbols of animal life, which the Egyptians had incorporated with their Divinities into more remote and purely poetical relations, as in the cases of Herè and Apollo.

XXVIII

By these and other such like devices, Homer gets rid of what, from proximity and wide extension, may have been the most formidable competitors with his Olympian figures. But the facts of purely local worship were, without doubt, too palpable for him

---

[1] This seems to be the only clear case. In several instances we have the expression *flox Hephaistoio.*

to overcome or overlook. The Olympian unity, which he was an agent, perhaps a main agent, in achieving, was the only unity that the case admitted, but it was a literary and political unity, probably most helpful in transmitting the religion, but not governing or superseding local or *pagan* usages, not without their counterpart in other religions. Hence, as to divine personages of an inferior order, like the Nymphs (*Od.* XIII. 356 *et alibi*), he does not interfere, but simply allows the facts to stand. We have, however, in Ithaca a sort of blurred picture, which seems at one moment to be Apollo, and at another Helios. Here he uses the artifice of avoiding nomenclature, and referring to the holiday as sacred to the ruling deity (*toio theoio, Od.* XXI. 258). We seem here to see the Olympian Apollo gradually effacing the old Nature-Power.

XXIX

On this subject there is no point more obscure than that which arises out of the twinship of Apollo and Artemis. In the Poems they are invested with resemblances sufficient for their relationship as brother and sister. But Artemis,

pure as well as beautiful, and thus in contrast
with Aphroditè, has not the lofty features which
lift Apollo above the merely Olympian level.
The anomaly offered by this twinship may have
for its explanation a joint worship of Sun and
Moon in the previously existing nature cult.
The light epithets which place Apollo in affinity
with a Sun - god have their analogue in the
Chrusenios and *Chruselakatè* of Artemis. And it
seems as if the distaff was assigned to her as in
correspondence with the bow of her brother. All
this relates to the Achaian and Olympian sphere.
Into a foreign sphere the Poet is too good a work-
man to carry his Achaian particularities. The
Artemis of the Theomachy is a Trojan goddess
and may represent a tradition of the all-producing
Earth like the later Ephesian Artemis. In this
view she is appropriately matched with Herè, in
whom we have the Hellenised form of the Earth
tradition, and who therefore chastises in her a
personal rival (*Il.* XXII. 489). The reproach of
Artemis to Apollo (*ibid.* 472), is appropriate not
to her sisterhood, but to her foreign attributes as
Nature-Power.

G

XXX

The position of Demeter in the Poems illus-
trates effectively the same vital element of the
system. It is evident from the later Eleusinian
tradition, and from the worship-chart of Pausanias,
where she stands fourth in the number of her
temples, that she was a great divinity in the local
cult of the Greek Peninsula. She seems to be
marked as elemental by the epithets *xanthe* and
euplokamos taken from the corn ; as we have in
Propertius *excutit et flavas aurea terra comas.*
Yet she is mentioned but seven times in the
Poems, and has no part in the action of the story,
Her name, as a form of Earth-Mother, *Gè Meter.*
appears to tell its own tale. She does not appear
among the Trojan party in the Theomachy ;
being probably the Earth-deity of the Peninsula
and not of the foreign sphere. The Trojans
worshipped Gaia (*Il.* III. 102-103).

XXXI

The high art of the Poet is nowhere more
notably exhibited than in his religious adjust-
ments. While endeavouring to subdue the exotic
traditions into his Olympian unity he avoids

such forms of proceeding as would have placed him
in sharp collision with them. It may be from
this cause, and in any case it appears to be the
fact, that where one of his deities has an exotic
background belonging to the old religion of the
country, he takes care not to place in the
Olympian court, which implies a governing office,
any other deity having similar attributes. Apollo
has a solar background, and accordingly Helios has
no place in the Achaian system. Herè is founded
on the Earth tradition ; so in like manner Demeter
becomes a purely negative personage. But in the
Theomachy, which is not an Achaian picture, the
actual duels are between competing claimants for
the same prerogative, Herè and Artemis as to the
Earth tradition ; Athenè and Arès (not yet a
naturalised Achaian divinity) as gods of war.

XXXII

The idea of Theanthropy is worked out not
only in the characters of divinities individually,
but in their political society ; which is made to
correspond with the established form of Achaian
polity on earth in its triform organisation. Zeus,
as its head, holds a position markedly analogous

to that of Agamemnon.   The Court or minor
assembly of Olympos is certainly called Agorè by
the Poet, but it corresponds to the *Boulè* or
Council of the higher Achaian chiefs.   The
greater assembly of *Il.* XX. corresponds with the
assembly of the army in Troas, of the people in
Ithaca.   It has before it the greatest question,
that of the part the gods themselves are personally
to take in settling the final crisis of Troy : as the
army is summoned to consider the Return in *Il.*
II. ; and as the Ithacan assembly in *Od.* XXIV.
treats of the situation created by the slaughter
of the Suitors.   This close correspondence, when
compared with the confusion of the Assyrian and
Egyptian mythologies, seems to exhibit in a vivid
light the symmetry of the Greek mind.

XXXIII

The researches of the last generation have
supplied materials for proving that Homer was
acquainted with Egyptian and Phœnician ideas,
and has largely dealt with them.   Yet more
recently, we have had similar evidence produced
with respect to Babylonian and Assyrian records.
It has also become plain that the Hebrew

traditions of the earliest Scripture were drawn from a source common to the ancestors of other nations as well as the Hebrews. There is thus no antecedent improbability that the ancestors of the Achaians had access to these venerable traditions before their separation from the common stock, and had transmitted them down to the contemporaries of the Poet ; although there is room on the other hand, at least at first sight, for the contention that these also were acquired through the medium of Phœnicia.

XXXIV

But the evidence of the Poems goes to show that the Achaian Greeks had some direct acquaintance with these primeval traditions. The Homeric conception of a Trine Government of the world, though moulded according to the exigencies of the Olympian system, is not without features of originality, tending to show that it may have been more than a mere copy from contemporary mythologies. Still less could he thus have found materials for his Apollo, who holds a great saving office, and whose will is identified with that of Zeus ; or for his Athenè, who represents the Supreme Wisdom afterwards conceived of, possibly on a traditional basis, as the *logos*. Without pursuing further the extraordinary attributes and prerogatives of these divinities in the Poems, it seems obvious that they correspond with the two great phases of the Messianic idea. The Iris of Homer is inexplicable except as an impersonation of the rainbow, conceived as that phenomenon is conceived in the Book of Genesis. His treatment of the serpent and the tree is closely analogous to the method in which he manipulates other exotic ideas, so as to bring them into correspondence with his theanthropic basis. Other particulars not few in number might be specified in detail.

XXXV

It may be remarked generally that, if the sources of many markedly Homeric presentations are to be found in the Hebrew traditions, or at the fountain-head from which those traditions may have been drawn, the mode of presentation is absolutely distinct, less ethical and spiritual, more imaginative and poetical. But we seem to trace in him at least remainders and tokens of many among the great moral conceptions, of which the early chapters of Genesis may be a parable as well as a history.

XXXVI

There is not found in the Homeric Poems any reminiscence which points either to the creation or the formation of the world or of the heavenly bodies, or to the succession of animated life upon this globe. There is no reference to the elements of which we are made, except in the line (*Il.* VII. 99), which signifies, that our bodies are to be resolved after death into earth and water. There are traces of a war in heaven, a rebellion in high places. There is a probable trace of the tradition of the Flood, so widely spread elsewhere.[1] The Poet gives no distinct record of anything like a golden age, but in two particular forms we have indications akin to those upon which it was founded. One is in some of the repeated references to the superior physical force possessed by the earlier generations of men. The other is in the divine descent of royalty at large, signified in his two remarkable epithets, *Diotrephes* and *Diogenes*, which correspond with the popular Egyptian tradition given by Herodotos.

XXXVII

Only in the Thearchy, not in human history or

---

[1] See *inf.*, the Essay at the close of the volume.

legend, have we a distinct recognition of prior periods, sharply severed from the present. Here we find—

1. The reference to Okeanos, as the source of all life: still severed, though in abdication, and having no tie of lineage with the present.

2. The reference to Kronos, parent or ancestor of Zeus, but deposed, and holding a position related to that of the alien and subdued powers, who pass by the name of Titans.

3. The recital of the convulsion in Olympos, in which the throne and liberty of Zeus were threatened, but through the resource and agency of Thetis (who represents both the old Nature dynasty and the new Hellenic ideas) an accommodation was effected, and the Thearchy securely established on the basis on which it appears in the Poems.

Also there are other minor indications.

XXXVIII

The two ideas in Homer that are really cardinal, central, generative, are the nation, and its reflection in the Thearchy, or Olympian society. All remaining subjects will be treated much more succinctly.

SECTION IV

RUDIMENTS OF ETHICS

I

WITH the progress of wealth and the multiplication of natural wants and comforts there grows up, as society becomes older, a new system of social ethics. Or rather, the preceding and more primitive system is both enlarged and braced in one of its provinces, while it is relaxed and lowered in others. If we take the three departments of good life as godly, righteous, and sober, or in other words as piety towards God, regard for relative rights, and the government of ourselves, morality may be found advancing under the second of these heads, at least in regard to property, while under the first and third of them it recedes. Such I conceive will be found to be the case with the morality of Greece in its classical age, as compared with the morality of the Achaian age represented in Homer.

II

The idea of sin, which is effaced from the thought and conscience, and even from the speech (so far as I know) of historic Greece, is powerfully though not perfectly represented in the Poems by the remarkable expression *atasthalié.*

Atasthalié does not signify merely a debilitated and disordered state of nature, or the victory of violent or seductive passion over opposing forces in man, but it means perverse, conscious, hardened, offending against an external law of righteousness.

Most curious is the treatment of this subject by Zeus in the divine assembly of the First *Odyssey*, where he says, " How do men accuse the gods ? for they say that from us proceed their woes ; but they also themselves through their *atasthaliai* have sorrows which come upon them despite of, and as overruling, the law of destiny." For destiny and its results he accepts the responsibility of a governor, but not for the further mischiefs imported into our lot by the element of a will of ours, independent and perverse.

III

In an altogether lower order of offence stands
the act of yielding to *Atè* the temptress, who is
ever busy among men : *atè, hē pantas aatai, Il.*
XIX. 91, 129. It is indeed a fault to yield, and
men must take the consequences of their fault,
as Agamemnon in the case of his offence against
Achilles (*ibid.* 137) ; but the gods have their re-
sponsibility, for Atè is the elder daughter of Zeus
(*ibid.* 91), who is himself sometimes a sufferer by
her deceiving arts (*ibid.* 126-129), though she is
not mentioned as acting upon deity except from
without. Agamemnon, while accepting the con-
sequences, seems to refer the blame to Zeus and
the higher powers, who introduced Atè within his
soul (*ibid.* 86-89).

IV

The Atasthalié of Homer seems to hold to his
Atè a relation resembling that between the *kakia*
and the *akrasia* of Aristotle : the one indicating
innate mischief, the other only inadequate means
of defence against evil when it solicits from with-
out. But neither of these have any reference to a

divine or objective law, whereas both the Homeric
conceptions have to do with the realities of religion ;
the greater one as a distinct and seemingly always
fatal and unpardoned offence, the other as a
liability occurring dimly, and not without the
concurrence or allowance of the gods.

V

If it be asked, in what relation do the Achaian
ethics stand to the Olympian gods ? the answer
will be complex and in the main unsatisfactory.
It is when the Poet refers to *theos* or *theoi* without
specification that the citation is usually made in the
interest of righteousness.   Chastity and purity as
such are not under the guardianship of the gods
personally made known to us ; but the precinct of
the family is very sacred as we perceive from the
quasi-personification of Histié, the hearth (*Od.*
XIV. 159).   And the poor, with the suppliant, are
placed everywhere under the protection of Zeus.
Collective morality, in the conduct of nations, is
more in the province of the gods than morality
merely personal.   But Homer places all morality
in connection with the supernatural order by the
sublime conception of the Eriniies, which degen-

erated, perhaps about the fifth century B.C., into the baser one of the Furies. In the *Hiketides* of Æschylus the transition is about taking place, and these singular personages are presented in both the competing characters — that is to say, as priestesses, so to speak, of the moral order, and as the avengers of crime.

VI

The ethical character of the Achaian civilisation is exhibited on its favourable side in the Poems by the following characteristics :—

1. The very high position assigned to women, and the purity and charm of the delineations of them.

2. The lofty conception of marriage, especially on the side of the wife.

3. The great strength of the family affections.

4. The absence from Achaian life of all the extreme forms of sin.

5. The stringency of the obligation to regard the suppliant, the stranger, and the poor.

6. The association established between piety towards the gods, and the sense of duty towards man (*Od.* VI. 120, 121).

7. The early development of a genuine courtesy and refinement in manners.

8. The strong habit of self-government, which implied regard and veneration for an internal standard or law of nature.

9. A marked deference in the individual to the moral judgments of the community (*Il.* IX. 459, 460) ascribed to a divine infusion.

10. The noble sense of political duty on the part of sovereigns, exhibited in the speech of Sarpedon to Glaukos (*Il.* XII. 310-322), and in the kingly rule of Odysseus.

11. With a strong sense of social enjoyment there was combined an aversion to excess. In the case of drunkenness this amounted to a sort of contempt towards it as involving degradation.

VII

In these capital respects there was, speaking generally, a decline in the ethical standard of classical Greece as compared with that of the heroic age. The large exhibition of Hebrew character in the Old Testament, which may with some latitude be called a contemporary exhibition, affords a better ground for comparison between Hebrews and Achaians, than pre-historic or remote · antiquity elsewhere supplies. So far as I am able to discern, the average Hebrew of the earlier historical Books of Scripture falls short of rather than exceeds in moral stature the Achaian Greek.

VIII

On the other hand, among the weaker points of Achaianism as compared with the classical time were these—

1. A low value set upon human life, so that the homicide, who has offended through passion, though he has to fly from the spot in order to escape from the vengeance of the relatives, yet obtains a reception elsewhere without difficulty.

2. Freebooting, presumably among strangers, is not held to be an offence.

3. Revenge for wrongs received is carried to a great or even brutal length, as by Achilles against the Trojans for the death of Patroclos, and by Odysseus in putting to death all the unchaste among the women-servants, who had had to attend on the Suitors in his absence.

4. If all kinds of wanton cruelty are absent on the one hand, neither do we find the quality of mercy, properly so called, on the other.

5. A vein of fraud with a view to gain in transactions is tacitly admitted even into high characters like that of Diomed, to wit in the exchange with Glaukos (*Il.* VI. 232-236).

SECTION V

I

THE politics of Homer contain ideas, hardly ex-
hibited elsewhere in a state of vitality and pro-
minence by the literature of the succeeding ages,
or of antiquity at large. These ideas seem like
a river which has sprung from its source in a
limestone country, and has again been buried in
the fissures of the rock ; but after a time it again
escapes from darkness into light, with its waters
clear as before. So the revived conceptions have
come to be incorporated in modern history.

II

First, the Poet sets a high value on the personal
freedom of the human being as such, and slavery

H

seems to wear in his eyes none of the sacredness
of an ancient established institution.   In the view
of Homer, apart from all incidental abuses (and
of these it must be admitted that we have no
pointed notice), it cripples and dwarfs the person
enslaved.   By the ordinance of God, says he, on
the day when a man becomes a slave he loses
half his manhood (*Od.* XVII. 322).   And it is
remarkable that when Achilles, worn and wearied
with the Underworld, would rather be in the
service even of a poor employer on the face of the
earth, it is in his service for hire, and not as a
slave (*Od.* XI. 489-491).   It seems that in his
emphatic condemnation of slavery the Poet has in
view not corporal suffering but moral results.

III

We have no case, in all the Poems, of the slave's
misery or the master's abuse of his power.

There is not found in them a purer character,
in point of piety or of relative duties, than
Eumaios, the *dios huphorbos* of the *Odyssey*, who
was kidnapped in his youth, and was the slave of
Odysseus.

Odysseus himself, at the proper time, kisses, on

the wrist, Dolios, the slave-gardener of Penelope (*Od.* XXIV. 398) ; the six sons of Dolios seized his hands (*ibid.* 410) ; and the whole family aided him in fight (497-499).

There are masters and slaves, but there is no community or class of masters as such, or slaves as such ; while there is a class distinction between the wealthy or well-to-do, *agathoi*, and the poorer, *cherëes* (*Od.* XV. 324). Slaves can possess property, and may, as in the case of Eumaios, hold other slaves. Familiarity between masters and domestic slaves has been known in modern times, and was carried to a high point in the Southern States of America; but it has prevailed much less as to predial slaves. There is no mention of slaves in the army before Troy.

IV

Another characteristic and singularly striking idea of the Poems is the power of the spoken word. It is a wonderful fact that, in those times, word and sword should stand together and in equal honour. It is the spoken word which agitates and sways and sometimes even converts the crowded assembly. The great epithet *kudi-*

aneira, glory-giving, is used exclusively for the *agorè* and the battle. In the *Odyssey* (VIII. 169-173) this gift seems to be treated as superior to beauty, even to godlike beauty. And, though we are probably closing the third millennium from Homer, the intervening time has produced no nobler specimens of oratory than some of those found in the Poems.

V

At that early stage in the social career of man, we find the oratory in the Poems singularly diversified. In the Trojan assemblies there is hardly a trace of the art. Among the Achaians, we have the bluntness of Aias, the chivalrous ardour of Diomed, so effective by downrightness and straightforwardness, the persuasive calmness of Nestor, the comprehensiveness and art of Odysseus, with perfect array of his resources, all strictly addressed to the end in view; the grandeur of Achilles, impassioned and almost Titanic, but ranging (to borrow a musical term) over the entire register of human feeling, and always checking emotion at the point where, through extravagance, it would become false in art.

Scope is given for the action of collective opinion first in the *Boulè* or Council ; where Agamemnon has a primacy, but nothing more. The speech of Nestor (*Il.* II. 29), advising concurrence in the scheme of Agamemnon, has the tone of an entirely free assent. In the critical meeting of *Il.* XIV. Odysseus sternly resists the device of Agamemnon (82 *seqq.*), who accepts the rebuke (*ibid.* 104) ; and Diomed will not hear of retreat.

The speeches made in the Assemblies are such as befit bodies which really deliberate. The speech of Thersites indeed is followed by blows from Odysseus, but the Poet is careful to record that the punishment inflicted had the approval of *Tis*. Now *Tis* is a *character* of great importance in the Poems. He is the impersonal representative of a dispassionate and free public opinion, collecting and expressing the sum of the case. And the existence of such a form of speech testifies to the habitual formation and expression of such opinion,

and shows that, even in the atmosphere of the
camp, there was a breath and flavour of liberty.
The mode of assent in an Assembly is manly
and becoming. In Ithaca a large party dissents,
and these quit the meeting (*Od.* XXIV. 464).
In the Assembly of *Il.* IX. 32, Diomed resists
outright the proposal of Agamemnon, declares
that, whatever others may do, he and Sthenelos
will remain, and carries the day against his chief
by the acclamation of the army (*ibid.* 50).

VIII

Mr. Grote has, by his notice,[1] given dignity to
a half verse, ascribed to Homer, but nowhere, so
far as is known, admitted by the Ancients into the
text. It ascribes to Agamemnon the power of life
and death. The possession of such a power would
have been in opposition to the pervading spirit of
the Poems throughout their whole extent. Had
it been genuine, this scrap of four words (*par gar
emoi thanatos*) would surely have found illustration
and support from some other portion of the text.
But there is no such thing in Homer, among the
proper instruments of government, as arbitrary

[1] *History of Greece*, vol. ii. p. 86, *n.*

power.   Power works in conjunction with reason.
On the other hand, civil authority is always treated
as flowing directly from Zeus, a fact which invests
it with sanctity, but which is entirely compatible
with its limitation.

IX

It is a seeming exception to the statement in
the last paragraph, that on the tumultuary disper-
sal of the Assembly in the Second *Iliad*, Odysseus,
in his bold struggle to rally and recall it, ex-
postulates with the chiefs, but strikes the common
soldier while upbraiding him (*Il.* II. 200).   This
however is a time of great and indeed desperate
straits, a time therefore of exception, when risks
have to be run ; and it is not the mere runaway
whom he treats thus roughly, but the runaway who
is also shouting to others in order to inflame the
panic.

X

The body politic, as we see it in the Poems, and
in the several princedoms or sovereignties, rather
than in the central primacy or supremacy, is a
regular organism, potentially complete ; but it is
so to speak in the gristle, not having hardened

into bone. Its rules of action are customary and unwritten. There is no such thing as law in the sense of something formulated and enacted ; and the word for it (*nomos*) is not found in the Poems. There are however fundamental though undefined principles, which are personified in the goddess Themis, and are habitually called *Themistes* in the Poems. They are the adamantine links of social order, and have in them a strong element of morality.

XI

This God-given power of rulers, which takes effect in action by means of counsel, has to do with priestly functions, at least within the Hellenic precinct. So Agamemnon presides at the sacrifice of the Poet in the Third *Iliad*, and Nestor at the festival of Poseidon in *Od.* III. Nor have we any mention of a priest at the Court of Alkinoos. The administration of justice between man and man was also a cardinal function of the sovereign. The language in *Il.* II. 201 and elsewhere seems as if it were personally exercised ; but in *Il.* XVIII. (497-508), on the Shield, the suit is tried by a body of elders as judges in the face of the people.

Thirdly, they had the duty of leadership in war ; and finally, they possessed endowments in land, which appertained to them as discharging these duties (*Il.* XII. 313). Kingship, even in Ithaca, brings wealth ; and Telemachos, in the event of surrendering it, looks to falling back upon the estate and the serfs whom Odysseus had obtained for him by predatory enterprise (*Od.* I. 392-398).

XII

. Between the Trojan and the Achaian assemblies there are marked distinctions. First, as has been remarked,[1] as to oratory. Secondly, there is nowhere an indication of differences in popular sentiment, and the supremacy of Hector seems to be unquestioned. Thirdly, the word commonly used to signify the acceptance by the people of what may have been proposed is *keladesan,* they rattled or clattered their assent : a term never applied to the decisions of the Achaian Assembly. Lastly, and perhaps most important of all, there is no *Tis,* no organ of a spontaneous, equitable, and pervading sentiment, of what we term a public opinion.

[1] *Supra,* V. p. 100.

SECTION VI

PLOT OF THE ILIAD

I

THE work of Homer, as an Epic poet, is to incor-
porate Beauty and Grandeur, and whatever most
harmonises with them, in living action. In the
place he has chosen for this purpose, it appears that
nationality, or patriotism, supplies his governing aim.
And if this be allowed, then I further submit that
the plot of the *Iliad* is a product of the nicest and
most consummate constructive art. It may almost
be said that Achaianism breathes in every line of
it ; nay that, in some marked forms of licence, this
idea modifies, though without subverting, the higher
laws of poetry. The Poet seeks to fashion his
country, to glorify his country, to make known his
country's crown in the highest developments of

character, to which human nature, by the means which were in his view, could reach.

II

While thus working intensely for Achaian nationality as a whole, the Poet does not forget local interests and feelings. He has contrived to incorporate in the movement of the *Iliad* a variety of scenes, which set forth the *aristeia* or prime performances of the several chieftains of principal rank. Arrangements of this kind are made first for Achilles not only in the closing books but in the whole structure of the Poem. Odysseus receives, even after allowing for his civil action in the Second Book and for his direction of the Doloneia, less than his share, but then he was to be amply compensated by becoming the protagonist of the sister Poem. Besides these, there are no less than six marked military presentations of as many different chieftains : Agamemnon, Diomed, Aias, Menelaos, Patroclos, and Idomeneus. This arrangement, setting aside the case of Patroclos, who is as a moon to set off the sun of Achilles, is admirably adapted to the territorial distribution of Greece before the Dorian conquest, and awards

to each population its due share of honour and
of pleasure, as an itinerating minstrel, dependent
on his art for subsistence, might be expected to
award them.

III

In this arrangement, so viewed, it may be said
that I only indicate a personal and interested
purpose ; but there seems to be a very high
poetical purpose also.   The colossal character of
Achilles requires the Poet to bridge over the
interval between him and common men.   The
intermediate grandeur of these personages, who
are as satellites placed around him, not only
sets off and enhances his surpassing magnitude,
but also helps to keep it within the bounds of the
natural.   Could we by laceration sever an Achilleis
from an Ilias, I believe the delineation of the great
hero would at once be more extravagant and less
effective ; would strain us more, and impress us
less.

IV

Considering Homer in his double relation, at
once to his subject and to his ‧auditory in the
Greek Peninsula, we perceive that the task he had

to perform was one requiring the most profound skill. He had to give to each and all of the Achaian warriors, who stood in the first class, a decisive predominance over such champions as Troy could set against them. For, unless he had rigidly observed this condition, he would have imparted a painful shock to national feeling. And yet he had to contrive that the Trojans as a body should reduce the Achaians, manifestly their superiors in war, to the last extremities, inasmuch as this was the only method by which Achilles could either be sufficiently glorified, or brought anew into the field to re-establish the fortunes of the enterprise.

V

It was also necessary that the Trojan warriors individually, while in each case palpably inferior, should, notwithstanding, not appear to be contemptible, but should be such that there would be credit in beating them. Nay, he had to invest Hector with such powers as would make him a presentable match for Achilles. And yet Hector, carefully observed through the vicissitudes of the field, is in reality inferior to all the Greek chieftains whom he has to encounter: to Aias, to Diomed, and (apart from the intervention of Apollo) to Patroclos. There is not a single Trojan chieftain who has the true Achaian fibre. We find it only among the allies of Troy, in the persons of Sarpedon and Glaukos; and it is evident that these, as Lycians, have some racial affinity with Greece. Nor is there a single case in which any Achaian of the first, or even the second order, is slain in fair fight by a Trojan. It is by the bow, and from the safe distance it allows, that the great Achaian chieftains are ingloriously disabled.

VI

To these difficult conditions the Poet has conformed, and I think with a perfect success, except in the case of Patroclos. Here the jealousy of Homer for Achaian honour has led him, as it appears to me, to the use of a clumsy expedient, which must be esteemed a poetical defect. Secondary aid from a divinity is one thing, as where Athenè, in XXII. 276, restores to Achilles the spear which he had launched. Her principal trick is to personate Deiphobos (XXII. 226), and to persuade Hector to fight by the hope of being

two to one. But against Patroclos Apollo actually
fights, so as to cripple and virtually almost destroy
him, after which he is wounded from behind by
Euphorbos, and nothing of substance remains for
Hector to do (*Il.* XVI. 791, 806, 850).

VII

There is not a single book of the *Iliad*, any
more than of the *Odyssey*, which, when judged by
the proper standard, is not found to be contributory
to its end. For example, the Doloneia or night-
raid of Book X. is wanted to give to Odysseus
such a share in the action as his greatness, and
especially his manysidedness, require. The con-
trivance is a double one, by which the diversified
feats of the Achaian warriors are at once ι to
exhibit their martial superiority, and yet to fail in
their main purpose of sustaining the cause, so that
they may create an overwhelming necessity for the
protagonist to encounter and overcome. The
more brilliant their performances are in themselves,
the more overpowering is the pre-eminence of him
who does what they cannot do. There is a subtlety
of adaptation in this arrangement such, as it may
not be easy to indicate in any other Epic.

VIII

Attention may be especially directed to the skill with which the case of Odysseus is treated in the *Iliad*. For this end let us consider what conditions were required. It was needful that he should in all things be worthy to be coupled with Achilles as a brother protagonist, and yet that he should not in any way compete with him, as such a rivalry would have marred the central purpose of the *Iliad*. It was needful also to leave to such warriors as Diomed and Aias a place second to none but the colossal warrior. Accordingly Odysseus is kept out of competition with them, and his great powers as a soldier are indicated rather than described. Yet he is the twin of a rth nearly superhuman : he is the many-minded, the all-accomplished, the never baffled. His surassing political energy is exhibited in the Second Book ; in the Ninth, his oratory ; in the Tenth his resources in the craft of war ; in the Twenty-Third his vast physical force. Even his peculiar strength of domestic affection is significantly exhibited in *Il.* II. 260 by his reference to his son, which has not any parallel in the Poem.

Homer differed from all, or almost all, epic poets in this, that he sang of men so much moi : than of things. This might probably be illustrated by showing what proportion of the lines in the *Ili. d* are thrown into speeches, and comparing it with t ? corresponding proportion in other Poems. But the case admits of a larger view. In the " Tale of Troy divine," Troy is wholly subservient. For Troy, and for the war of Troy, the Poem has no beginning, and no ending. Not so for the glory and character of the " man " whose "wrath " the Poet sang. It is as if he had had a forethought of the painter's and the sculptor's secret, that the consummation and perfection of their work lie in the human form.

X

The greatest among the structural peculiarities of the *Iliad* is the twofold and parallel movemei,; of the Olympian and the human agencies, eačl· of them so fully developed in speech, individua. character, and action, that either might almost be conceived of as an Epic in itself without the other ; so complete in each is the elaboration of the parts, and the determination of their relation to the whole.

SECTION VII

THE GEOGRAPHY OF THE POEMS

I

THE Geography of the Poems, and of the *Odyssey* in particular, is not a mere question of delimitations upon the surface of the earth, but is a key to their ethnography, which in its turn is a key to manners and religion, in a word to the most central part of their contents. This geography of the *Odyssey* has been thoroughly vitiated and obscured by the action of spurious Latin tradition, which forcibly accommodated Homer to the exigencies of a Roman dynasty and a South Italian Poem. In this manner the scheme of the *Odyssey* has been reduced from a basis which, though indeterminate, is, when viewed with due reference to the circumstances of the Poet and his means of information, entirely rational, to a tissue not only of fable but of something near absurdity.

II

It may be well to select a case, in order to illustrate the determined recklessness of the Latin representations of Odyssean geography. It habitually identifies the island of Aiolos (*Od.* X. 1) with Stromboli. Now in the way of such an identification there stand the following facts :

1. From this island, a continuance of Zephuros, say N.N.W. wind, carries the ship straight homewards until it has sighted Ithaca ; that is to say, right across the Italian Peninsula.

2. The island of Aiolos is one, and apparently solitary ; whereas the Lipari islands are many.

3. Stromboli is mentioned without either mountain or volcano, a double objection for any one who has passed by it at sea, since, to the eye of the voyager, it is simply a volcanic mountain, with nothing else projecting from the main.

4. The time given is nine days and nights from the Cyclop-land. But, as the same tradition places that land in Sicily, the time allowed is incompatible with other adjustments between space

and time, such as the five days from Crete to Egypt, nearly double the distance as the crow flies.

III

The geography of the *Iliad* may be said to have generally the same limits as the personal experience of Homer, if we may include in that phrase, together with what he had seen, what he had the means of learning from adequate, easy, and diversified sources of information. There will still be exceptions ; as in the noteworthy survey by Zeus of the country beyond the Balkans in *Il.* XIII. 3-6 (which probably illustrates the far-reaching action of the god), and the reference in II. 857 to the silver mines of Alubè. The Poet may personally have had a coast knowledge of Western Asia Minor, and the text of the Trojan Catalogue pretends to no more. He was probably acquainted with the plain of Troy, but in a loose manner : for the descriptions, while they are stamped with local features, and highly picturesque, have not been shown to be accurate.

IV

Schliemann has argued, with high probability,

that the site of Troy was on the hill of Hissarlik.[1]
This argument is favoured by one, or more, marked
indications of the text.   But it is understood that
there are to be further excavations, under the
same generous auspices, with a view to more
ample means of judgment.   Meantime the field of
choice has been narrowed.   Eckenbrecher has
proved to a demonstration that the site was not,
according to the evidence of the Poems, on the
rock of Bounarbashi,[2] as it had been somewhat
fashionable to assume.

V

It will be allowed on all hands that the geo-
graphy peculiar to the *Odyssey* in the voyages of
Odysseus has no relation whatever to the personal
experience of the Poet, unless it be within the
limit of the Odyssean dominions.   It thus happens
to be very nearly the fact that each of the Poems
has a geography to itself.

For the sake of convenience I term the precinct

---

[1] *Troy and its Remains*, by Dr. Henry Schliemann, Murray, 1875;
Homeric Synchronism, by W. E. G., pp. 22-31.

[2] *Die Lage des Homerischen Troja*, Düsseldorf, 1875; *Ueber
die Lage des Homerischen Ilion*, in the Rheinisches Museum, 1842;
Homeric Synchronism, p. 22.

of the Iliadic geography the Inner Zone, and the
peculiar sphere of the *Odyssey* the Outer Zone.

VI

An important subdivision, belonging to the Inner
Zone, is presented by the dominions of Odysseus.
They are in four provinces or departments : Douli-
chion, Samè, Zante, and Ithaca. The Doulichian
force is placed under Meges in *Il.* II. 625-630,
but the Doulichian Suitors, though only a selection,
constitute half the entire number of those gathered
in Ithaca. The Poems nowhere describe Douli-
chion and Samè as separate islands. I construe
them to be portions of what is now Cephalonia,
divided physically and socially in the midst by
the bay of Samè and a neck of mountain land.
Here the name Dulichi still subsists, and the
position agrees fairly well with the expression of
Homer "over against Elis." Zante requires no
comment. The remarkable harbour of Ithaca is
well described in *Od.* XIII. 96-101, as is the
general contour and character of the island in
other passages.

VII

As the Phœnicians were the only navigators
known to Homer who frequented either the
Euxine, or the Mediterranean westwards of Greece,
with the Ocean lying beyond, we are led at once
to the inference that the mariners of this race must
have been the sources of his information as to the
geography of the Outer Zone, and that his informa-
tion could only have been oral.   Oral information
on geographical sites and distances, unchecked by
visible delineations, or by general knowledge of
the distribution of land and sea, were of necessity
subject to much misapprehension ; while the nar-
rators, dealing with one who was at their mercy,
had the double temptation, on the one hand, of
indulging in the marvellous, and on the other, of
so dressing their relations as not to invite possible
competitors into the regions from whence they
drew exclusive gains.

VIII

Moreover, as practical rather than scientific
mariners, they could only speak in general terms ;
their narratives could hardly be consistent one with

another ; marked natural features would be easily
reported and remembered, yet without any adequate
means of fixing relative situation, and with a great
risk of amalgamating locally indications existing
at more than one place. We have also to bear
in mind that, in the state of knowledge then sub-
sisting, descriptions would sometimes mislead on
account of their very truthfulness in referring to
one and the same region contradictory phenomena,
which were indeed to be found there, but at different
times. Thus Homer had evidently been informed
that perpetual day, and also perpetual night, were
characteristics of the north. The only expedient
open to him was to interpose a great distance
between his Laistrugonians of the double day, and
his Kimmerians of the unending night. So again,
the accounts he would probably pick up of the
Bosporos, the Straits of Messina, and the Straits
of Gibraltar, would readily, and almost inevitably,
tend to fuse themselves in his mind into one de-
scription. A narrow sea-passage, a current through
it, and more or less of rocky shore, form the essence
in each case. And they were likely to run together
at the local point which, from any cause, had
most deeply impressed the mind of the Poet.

IX

With these formidable difficulties the Poet struggles as best he may, and exhibits an ingenuity which is in thorough keeping with his higher gifts. It is remarkable, considering the nature of the task and the scantiness of the resources, that the whole narrative he has woven together does not contain any gross inconsistency as to its general structure. Where he is at fault he simply, instead of giving particulars, leaves us an *hiatus*. Thus at several points of the great circuit we find ourselves wholly without guidance. But this lapse into silence bears witness to the importance of the indications, in the cases where he has supplied them.

X

And, in truth, he has contrived to furnish many such tokens, which are for the most part utterly disregarded in the Latin identifications. They are contrived as follows—

1. As to direction, by naming the winds, by the sun, and in one instance by the stars (*Od.* V. 270-277).

2. As to distance, by weather, and by the mode

of locomotion, which is either sailing, or rowing, or floating on a raft, or swimming, together with the number of days occupied in the several operations.

3. As to latitude, or distance northward, this is conveyed through a change of climate indicated by the use of fires otherwise than for food. See particularly the great fire of the cavern of Kalupso (*Od.* V. 59), where there was no cooking.

4. As to the identification of spots, by specifying marked local features, as in the form of the island of Thrinakiè, and in the harbour of the Laistrugones.

XI

The chief winds of Homer are Boreas and Zephuros. Euros and Notos fill a smaller space in the action. But these four winds do not closely correspond with the four chief points of the compass, as North, South, East, and West. Zephuros is from W. northwards, and Boreas from N. principally eastwards. Zephuros is the best defined, Euros and Notos very indeterminate, but all seem to cover at least several points of the compass. The indications from sunset and sunrise in like manner may be understood to range over an arc of the horizon corresponding with the variations at different seasons.

XII

The voyage of Odysseus in the Outer Zone may be taken to commence with his passing the Malean Cape, and to close either upon the border-land of Scheriè, or upon the voyage to Ithaca, which is represented vaguely as covering a large distance.   The several stages are :—

1. Land of the Lotophagoi.
2. Land of the Kuklopes.
3. Island of Aiolos.
4. Laistrugoniè.
5. Aiaiè, the island of Kirké.
6. The Underworld.
7. Aiaiè, on his return.
8. Island of Thrinakiè.
9. Ogugiè, the island of Kalupso.
10. Scheriè, the land of the Phaiakes.

XIII

The indications given by Homer, as to the situation of the several spots which mark the stages, do not in all cases admit of verification. It is only surprising that there is not more of obscurity and confusion.   Among cardinal points, as conceived and arranged in the brain of Homer, which can be established by reasoning from the text, I place the following :—

1. The land of the Kuklopes is in the south.

2. The island of Aiolos lies to the north of west from Ithaca.

3. The island of Calupso is in the far north.

4. Laistrugoniè is also northern.

5. Aiaiè lies to the eastward, and perhaps north of east.   But the site is vaguely conceived.

6. Thrinakiè, with Scylla and Charybdis, lies between Aiaiè and Greece, on the way homeward.

7. Northward of the Greek Peninsula, there lies (not the mass of the European continent but) a great expanse of sea.

8. There is no trace of the existence of Italy to be found in the Poems.

XIV

If these propositions be sound, their combined effect will be to draw in rough outline the voyage of Odysseus.   It is begun under the influence of Boreas, and the route lies by the south-west to the west, north-west, north, and then south-eastward to the island of Thrinakiè, lying east of Greece. From this point he is driven back to Ogugiè in the far north ; and then brought over sea, by the longest of his passages, to Scheriè.

The voyage so viewed occupies about three-quarters of , the whole compass of the horizon. The remaining quarter is covered by the tour of Menelaos, as it is summarily described in *Od.* IV. 81-86.

XV

Scheriè is almost conclusively identified with Corfù by the account given in *Od.* V. 281 of its aspect from the north, as that of a shield, a nearly level line along the sea, with a boss or upward projection. The northern coast of the island lies rather low, with the very marked exception of Mount San Salvador, which at a single point rises to a height of near 3000 feet. Both the representation and the reality are peculiar, and the resemblance is exact, except in a single particular, namely, that the " boss " on the line of coast is not in the middle, but towards the eastern end. Homer's idea of Scheriè was probably derived from report, and is much less precise than his account of Ithaca ; but it appears reasonably to suffice for identification.

XVI

The interesting question remains, What was Homer's idea of the figure into which the surface of the earth, so largely conceived by him, was cast? This might perhaps be called his geotypy.

It seems a mistake to suppose he thought the earth was like a plate, although undoubtedly he conceived that it had bounds, which were supplied by the great river Okeanos. He plainly believed that the Underworld lay beneath the ground on which we walk, and at no immeasurable distance from it. He believed also that access to the Underworld was to be had by passing to the extremity of the land in an eastern region, and then crossing Okeanos. Finally, the sun, in his course from one day to another, passed over the mouth of the Underworld, so that he could threaten (*Od.* XII. 382, 383) if offended to stop, or enter in, and shine there. Apparently the conception of the Poet concerning the earth approximated to the idea of sphericity, but we should perhaps suppose a slice cut off from the lower side.

On the Points of Contact between the Assyrian Tablets and the Homeric Text

THE picture of the Homeric world, belonging to the period when legend hardens into history, lies within the range of that comparative science which of late has done so much to illuminate antiquity. But we step beyond the process of collecting and comparing allied phenomena, when circumstances enable us to arrange them in order of time, or to connect them, such as they appear in one country, by affiliation, with their yet older forms manifested in another.

To this purpose, the condition of Homeric Greece is eminently favourable. Although the Greek Peninsula is surrounded at all points of the circle by masses of land as well as sea, all the solid and operative traditions of the Poems, all that exercised an influence in developing the nation, came from within one-fourth part of that circumference, lying to the South and South East, and came over sea with the ships of the Phœnicians. We are thus directed by geographical indications to certain quarters, and especially to Syria, Assyria, and Egypt. By the aid of Egyptian discoveries, it has been found possible to trace into that country much that we find in the Poems, and to draw from the connection thus established some . lights that help to clear the early history of Greece.[1] And the time seems now to have arrived, when it may be reasonably attempted to show, from the Babylonian and Assyrian monuments, how numerous appear to be the points of contact between them and the Homeric text. Apart from the wider investigations of comparative science, it is matter of legitimate interest to trace upwards to their source, through the channels now opened, a portion at least of the influences which have operated in moulding the Greek nation, and thus somewhat to advance at a point of capital interest the important work, now in progress, of reconstituting piecemeal the earlier records of our race.

I have already made some slight efforts in this

---

[1] Lauth, *Homer und Ægypten; Homeric Synchronism*, 1876, part ii.

province of inquiry ;[1] but increased knowledge is now accessible, and with it increased evidence of Babylonian derivation. In particular, the points are numerous, which appear to associate the indications of the Poems with the Babylonian cosmogonies and theological systems. Those indications indeed are not abundant. The simple and healthy realism of Homer indisposed him alike to physics and to metaphysics. But, as respects the origin of things, Homer has given us at least one decisive indication. The great encircling river Okeanos is the parent of the gods themselves (*Il.* XIV. 301, 302) and of their entire number (*ibid.* 245); or, in other words, water is the origin of all things. Hence, no doubt, it is that this ancient and venerable, though purely elemental, Power is treated by the Poet with such singular respect, and is not called, like the other elemental powers, to appear in the great Olympian Assembly (*Il.* XX. 7), where with them he would only have taken a secondary rank.

Now it is *a priori* most unlikely that this could have been an original conception of the Poet's brain. The Poems are intensely pervaded by the theanthropic principle, and at all points they

[1] *Homeric Synchronism*, pp. 230, 234.

K

depress and repel merely elemental conceptions.
To place, therefore, an elemental personage in the
relation of parent to all the ruling divinities is
therefore a somewhat gross anomaly. The
force of this idea will be most clearly seen, if we
bear in mind how venerable in Homer's eyes were
parentage and seniority—

οἶσθ' ὡς πρεσβυτέροισιν 'Ερίννες αἰὲν ἕπονται.[1]

And again in the light of the shift, to which the
Poet has been driven in order to save at once
his general principle and the integrity of this
particular conception. For surely it is a shift
to save the dignity of Okeanos by excluding him
from the divine assembly. It was likely, then, that
the notion of an oceanic origin of things came
to him from a foreign source, and from a foreign
source such as would invest it in his eyes with
something of authority and sanctity. This con-
dition in all likelihood would for him be supplied
by a Babylonian stamp.

The entire tenour of the Poems bears witness
to the reverence of Homer for the past. Such
reverence could not be confined within the geo-
graphical limits of his own country. So the

[1] *Il.* XV. 204.

doctrine of oceanic origin, which is incongruous in relation to the Olympian system and the theanthropic principle, can readily and naturally be accounted for as a Phœnician importation from Babylonia ; and, alike from the evidence of the monument and from the records of later times, we learn how the conception of a water origin of things prevailed in the Babylonian system.

It is, perhaps, with some reference to this primary conception, that Homer has given us an isolated and seemingly casual utterance in the line (*Il.* VII. 99) which appears to refer the composition of the human frame to the elements of earth and water. Menelaos speaks of the Greek chiefs, in their momentary hesitation to accept the challenge of Hector, as physically doomed to pass at death into these elements—

ἀλλ' ὑμεῖς μὲν πάντες ὕδωρ καὶ γαῖα γένοισθε.

There is nothing in the Poems to associate this notion of aqueous origin with the Kronid dynasty of deities, either by explaining the manner, or by detailing the stages, of the derivation. I add however some words cited by Dr. Driver[1] from the Assyrian tablets—

[1] In the *Expositor*, No. XIII. p. 39. Also Sayce, *Hibbert Lectures*, p. 384.

"When as yet the heaven above had not declared,
Nor the earth beneath had recorded a name,
The august ocean was their generator,
The surging deep was she that bare them all.

. . . . .

When of the gods none had yet issued forth,
Or recorded a name, or fixed a destiny,
Then were the great gods formed."

I turn now to the subject of mythological relations between Olympian, and Babylonian or Assyrian divinities.

In all attempts to trace, in a deity of a particular system and country, a thread of historical derivation from a deity of another name, belonging to another system and country, it is to be borne in mind that the names and attributes of such deities are subjected to change in a manner and degree totally unknown within the precincts of those other religions which have carried upon them, from their origin onwards, a characteristic stamp capable of certifying their identity throughout all ages. Such are the Christian, Jewish, and Mahometan religions.

It is indeed possible in such cases that, while the stamp remains intact, and in the absence of any violent breach with the current traditions of the system, its character and effect may suffer from within important and even essential changes. But this is alteration within definite dividing lines, alteration without mixture. In earlier days, the silent causes of disintegration were actively at work ; but there were others to boot. There were constant migrations and conquests, settlements and resettlements, displacements and coalitions of the populations ; the religions underwent along with them perpetual modifications, and shifted, like a kaleidoscope, from time to time, in the combinations which they presented. In the competitions of languages caused by new arrivals, names are changed ; and competing worships give and take, and arrive by intercommunication at a kind of *concordatum*. Such a result, in satisfying the demands of social peace, disfigures or transfigures, again and again, the religious traditions of a country ; or breaks them up into a multitude of local worships, liable to be unsettled afresh by the neutralising schemes which may have been devised and prosecuted in their own interests by sovereigns and priesthoods. To all the difficulties produced by these causes are to be added the absence or imperfection of record. Apart from this last source of embarrassment, the picture presented by

Babylonian and Assyrian religion may perhaps be compared to the network of those Norfolk and Suffolk rivers, which join and part, and rejoin and part again, so as to defy or greatly hamper any clear continuous tracing of their several identities.

Subject to the full force of the preceding observations, it seems safe to say that the Poseidon of Homer carries marks, which are highly probable if not demonstrative, of Babylonian association.

In the Poems, he presents to us traits of Southern and of Eastern derivation ; for example in the following points, the detailed proof of which has of course to be given in its proper place, where the needful details would be permissible.

1. As the god of the Phœnicians.
2. As the god of the Aithiopes.
3. As the father of the Kuklopes.
4. As the god of the horse.
5. As the dark-haired god.
6. As resting on the Solyman mountains.
7. As related to the Giants.

But the Aithiopes stretch from the rising to the setting sun ; and all these indications taken together do not suffice to mark any one particular region of the South and South-east, from which the

Poseidonian tradition was derived. Let us see, however, whether there are not some grounds for supposing that it may have been partially at least borne upon that stream of report, which from the Persian Gulf passed into Syria, and then by the Mediterranean into Greece.

It seems evident that some important tradition connected with the sea found its way from Chaldæa into Greece : because Thalassa (or Thalatta), their name for the sea, is of Chaldæan origin.

Again, the position of Poseidon is peculiar in this that he is the god of the sea, and yet is not an elemental god. He has a palace in the sea-hollows, but he does not inhabit the sea like Nereus, and he seems to appear in Olympos (*Od.* XIII. 125-160), and moves constantly and variously on the surface of the earth. The correspondence is here very strong between him and the Ea or. Hea of the Babylonian Triad. That name is pre-Semitic, and Hea belongs to Eridu on the Persian Gulf, the earliest seat of the Chaldæan civilisation (Sayce, *Hibbert Lectures*, p. 104). Within his local sphere he was supreme, the supreme god of his country. It is probably in this character that Merodach is the son of Ea. And so Poseidon likewise bears upon him the notes of having been supreme in his country of origin, a Zeus-Poseidon, as Aidoneus was the Zeus *catachthonios.* Hence it may be that Poseidon exhibits in Homer a constant tendency to set himself up as a match for Zeus. It is with the utmost difficulty that Iris induces him to obey the command which requires him to quit the Trojan plain (*Il.* XV. 200-207); and in the *Odyssey,* where he persecuted the hero against the wish of the whole Thearchy, Zeus says no more than that he surely will not persevere (which however he does) in defiance of the entire body of the gods (*Od.* I. 78).

One of the most characteristic notes of the Homeric Poseidon is his complexion, as the dark or black Poseidon. This is not only indicated by epithet : the word *Kuanochaites* or dark-haired (*Il.* XX. 144), stands substantively to describe him, without any other name or epithet. With this we have to compare the Hymn which treats Ea as the creator of the black race, meaning the old non-Semitic population belonging to Eridu (Sayce, pp. 142, 143). There is no other appropriation in Homer of an epithet of colour to a divinity which resembles that given in the case of Poseidon.

In one point the representation of Poseidon (*ibid.* p. 131) is markedly different from that of Ea ; this, namely that Ea was the god of wisdom. This may mean little more than that Eridu was the first known seat of civilisation, and that Ea was the god of Eridu. Certainly there is here no mark or resemblance to Poseidon, who represents nothing but the conception of mere force. But then the particular attributes of different deities continually shifted with the courses of social change ; and the feature of wisdom may have been effaced from the portraiture of Ea at some period before any reflection of it was conveyed into the Syrian, Phœnician, and Olympian systems ; or he may have been blended with another form of the tradition ruling westwards, and presenting the rude and brutal character to be expected (*Od.* VII. 56-60, 205, 206), in the father of the Kuklopes, the kinsman of the Giants, and the object, in historic times, of worship by human sacrifices.

Again : In Babylonia we find the earliest source of the legends of human deification, and in association with this, of the gigantic size and strength of primeval man. Izdubar has already mounted into heaven. Leucothiè, our only case of pure deification in Homer (*Od.* V. 335), meets us in the Outer Zone. These legends are associated by Lenormant with the remarkable passages in Genesis (Gen. vi. 1, 2, also 4), which, as he holds, describe the monstrous preterhuman births from sons of God and daughters of men, and which state that the Nephilim, rendered giants, were in the earth in those days (*Origines de l'Histoire*, p. 334). Now Ea is the great deity, whom alone we can trace even from the Persian Gulf into the Olympian Thearchy, and whose counterpart we find in Poseidon. But the Poseidon of Homer stands in immediate relation to these Nephilim. The Cyclop Poluphemos is his son. Nausithoos also sprang from him, by a human mother, who was herself the daughter of Eurumedon, King of the Giants, and the mother of Alkinoos, King of the Phaiakes (*Od.* VII. 56-66). These were related to the gods, like the Kuklopes and the impious and savage Giants (VII. 205). So again the gigantic Laistrugones, and the deified Leucothiè belong to the sea-domain (*Od.* X. 120). Thus we have new ties between Poseidon and the home of Ea.

We have yet another connecting link between

Ea, the offspring of the Persian Gulf, and Poseidon. Evidently, in Homer's eyes, the Persian Gulf was part of the Ocean-stream, coiled around the world. For in *Il.* I. 423 he places his Aithiopes upon the Ocean verge. True, they are visited, in that passage, not by Poseidon only but by the whole body of the gods. But the visit paid to these same Aithiopes in *Od.* I. 22-25, was paid by Poseidon alone. The indication seems to be first of a relation between the Olympian religion and these southern people, as having supplied some at least of its elements ; and secondly, of a more special relation between them and Poseidon. Who then were these Aithiopes ? It seems more than probable that they were, at least in their eastern branch, the Babylonian Assyrians ; for these only, so far as we know, could fulfil that condition of Homer's description, which placed them on the River Okeanos. It will be remembered that Menelaos, after his tour, which extended to an eighth year, enumerates the countries he had visited, not without some attempt at geographical combination. He gives first Kupros, Phoinikè, the Egyptians. These may be considered as exhibiting a comparatively usual route. He then mentions another group of three countries and races.

Αἰθίοπάς θ' ἱκόμην καὶ Σιδονίους καὶ Ἐρεμβούς.

He finally describes Libya, in the next line, by a mark of its own. In the line I have quoted, the Sidonians are appropriately mentioned. Sidon was in Homer's time the chief state of Phœnicia, and best represents its intercourse and traffic with the East. The *Eremboi* are doubtless the Arabs, and it thus seems that these *Aithiopes* can hardly be other than their neighbours the Babylonian Assyrians. Through their medium then, and through the location assigned to them on the River Ocean, we seem to have Poseidon placed once more in apparent derivation from the Babylonian Ea, who came from Eridu on the Persian Gulf.

While, however, I think it to be beyond doubt that the Babylonian Ea, or Hea, is principally represented for Achaian purposes by Poseidon, I do not wholly dissent from the opinion of those who hold that he is represented in Kronos. For Kronos is directly associated with the rebellious Titans (*Il.* XIV. 274-279), who dwell in his company below the ground, therefore in a portion of the Underworld ; and indeed below Tartaros, its deepest region (*Il.* VIII. 14), and the operation of placing them there is performed at the extremity of the earth or land (*Il.* XIV. 200-205), which we have reason to connect with the Aithiopes and Babylonia. We must not be startled at this change from a singular to a dual form of the tradition. The severance may have taken place in the local divisions of Babylonia itself ; and we must remember that the Babylonian doctrines could only come to Homer piecemeal, and as it were in tatters, by oral report, and often without connecting links save such as the insight of his genius could imagine.

There is another not less characteristically marked relation established, apparently, by the monuments ; namely, the relation between the Ishtar of the Babylonians and Assyrians, and the Aphroditè of Homer.

The Homeric Aphroditè offers to us a picture so remarkable as almost absolutely to require that we should refer it to some historical source, which may serve to account for, if not to reconcile, the incongruous elements which it presents to us. Let me briefly note some of these particulars. In the first place, she is evidently a foreign goddess, who as such has little claim on the reverence of the Poet. She is related to Cyprus and Cytherè, and we must therefore take it for granted that her worship was established in those islands. But we have no sign that it had in Homer's time found its way into the Greek continent. Still she was, in her own person, the acknowledged model of form. As Pallas represented the unattainable in art and skill, so Aphroditè exhibited it in beauty (*Il.* IX. 389, 390). But it is evident throughout that her power lies only in the region of sense. She supplies Herè with the means of stirring up lust in Zeus ; she bestows the same baleful gift on Parïs (*Il.* XXIV. 30) ; she drives Helen into the arms of her paramour, and is taunted by her, and by Athenè, as the great pander of the world (*Il.* III. 400, V. 42). And though she is placed in a certain special relation to nuptials, this, we may plainly see, is only on the fleshly side (*Il.* V. 429 ; *Od.* XX. 73). So it is that the loveliest of all visible temples, the female form, is dedicated to a foul demon. There is not a single trace of a moral element in her character. This combination is evidently revolting to the Poet ; so that he habitually exhibits the goddess as odious or contemptible. Nay, he will not allow her to be supreme even over corporeal Beauty ; for, in the case of the daughters of Pandareus, it is Herè who gives them loveliness, and Artemis stature, while the office of Aphroditè is to supply them with cheese, honey, and soft wine (*Od.* XX. 68-71). She is corporally punished both by Diomed in battle, and by Athenè in the Theomachy, in which however she appears only as an interloper. She is not honoured with a place among the combatants (*Il.* XXI. 416-426). The poet evidently would not present her as a match for any one among his recognised Hellenic deities. On examining this picture as a whole we are compelled to say the original, from which it was drawn, must have been of a peculiar character, and to ask where it was to be found ? I conceive that it was not a copy, but a reproduction which had been subjected to the modifications required by the ideas of the Poet and his nation.

It has long been familiarly known that we are to look to Syria and the East as the region in which was fully accomplished, by a sort of spurious consecration, the baleful union between unrestrained lust and the observances of divine worship. On the one side there was the image of perfect beauty, on the other the sensual appetite associated with a frightful disregard of all boundary and measure, of the structure of the family, and of the laws of nature. Against the suggestions thus conveyed, the Poems of Homer form a noble protest ; and it is only in the mildest shape, and under the veil which is of itself a confession, that we find exhibited in Achaian life this touch of human infirmity. The conception of what is thoroughly and entirely dissolute, embodied some of the forms in which Ishtar has been worshipped, was in her associated not only with divinity but with paramount rank among divinities. She was the only goddess who had a place in the Assyrian system by the side of Asshur (Sayce, *Hibbert Lectures*, p. 123) ; and in the Old Testament and Phœnicia, as Ashtoreth, she ranks not less high than Baal. It is noteworthy that, while Phœnician immigration could not but bring her worship into Greece, at least she did not come there vested with the attributes of supremacy. Shorn not of her sensuous beauty but of her supreme rank, she enters the Olympian assembly in its lowest and least honoured grade : and Homer may have been in a degree the cause of what is at any rate to all appearance a fact, that the Aphroditè worship did not very greatly spread in many parts of historic Greece. Pausanias assigns to her thirty-seven temples and shrines in his Attic, Corinthian, and Arcadian sections ; but only seventeen in all the rest of the country.

Great obscurity overhangs the origin of Ishtar as a deity. Nor can we wonder if it was found no simple process to promote to so high a place a conception in which the impure ingredients were found so greatly to preponderate. What was good in it passed over to the pale and ineffectual tradition of the *Aphroditè Ourania :* in Asia, the coarser elements alone became widely and permanently operative.

As recorded on the tablets, the doings of Ishtar have imposed reserve upon Mr. G. Smith. He says, " In the succeeding lines, various amours of Ishtar are described. These I do not give, as their details are not suited for general reading " (*Assyrian Discoveries*, p. 178). She offers her love to Izdubar, but is repelled, and complains to her father Anu :

L

"Father, Izdubar hates me,
Izdubar despises my beauty,
My beauty and my charms."

And she asks Anu to create a winged bull to be the instrument of her vengeance accordingly.

Another remarkable though limited correspondence with the Babylonian system is to be found in one of the epithets applied by the Homeric text to Aïdoneus. He is called by Homer *pulartes*, the gate - fastener. Elsewhere in the Poems, the word appears as a proper name, taken no doubt from the office of a gate-keeper. As an epithet, it is applied only to Aïdoneus (*Il.* VIII. 367 ; XIII. 415 ; *Od.* XI. 277), and always in conjunction with the word *krateros*, signifying his might. Now the "gates of hell" supply a common figure, expressive of strength, but without any very special point or significance, and it long remained an unsolved riddle to interpret *pulartes*, for it is far from evident at first sight why the king of the Underworld should be his own porter.

Now the legend of Ishtar's descent to the Underworld appears to supply a pretty complete explanation : which is all the more wanted because the rather elaborate description of the Underworld in the *Odyssey* makes no reference whatever to any gates. There are, indeed, gates of Tartaros, which have the characteristics of a prison. But Tartaros was not within the limits of Hades, which alone appears to have constituted the realm of Aïdoneus (see *Il.* VIII. 15, 16, and XV. 188). That region is to all appearance modelled to some extent upon Egyptian ideas. Now, in the Egyptian *Book of the Dead*, there is a representation of a gate, that is to say of folding doors, but, so far as I have learned, they stand open,[1] and cannot possibly have suggested the epithet we are examining. And the common idea of Hades is rather the all-devouring, and therefore open, than the all-imprisoning, and therefore shut. But, according to the Assyrian tablets, the gates of the Under-world are an elaborate and principal part of its equipment. We derive our knowledge of the particulars from the descent made into it by Ishtar (Sayce, *Hibbert Lectures*, IV. p. 221, *seqq.*) when in quest of the healing waters which were to restore Tammuz to life. The Assyrian Under-world is not here the all-receiving, but " the house

---

[1] *Book of the Dead.* Printed for the British Museum, 1890. Introduction, p. 12.

from within which there is no exit" (Smith,
Assyrian Discoveries, p. 220).

"The passage to these subterranean abodes is
through the seven gates of the world, each guarded
by its porter, who admits the dead, stripping him
of his apparel, but never allowing him to pass
through them again to the upper world" (Sayce,
Hibbert Lectures, p. 364).

Ishtar threatens the gate-keeper in order to
procure entrance into Hades. At each of the
seven gates, she has to deposit a portion of her
ornamentation, in conformity with the rules of the
place, and the orders of its queen Allat. It may
be conjectured that the purpose of this operation
was to secure her withdrawal after the transaction
of the business on which she had come. The
account of it is given in language sufficiently
obscure : but it seems to be completed (Sayce, *ubi
Sup.*) when the waters of life are poured upon
her ; and, as she retraces her steps to the upper
world, Namtar the agent of Allat restores to her,
at each of the gates successively, the attire and
ornaments of which she had been divested. These
gates with their fastenings are thus a principal,
and perhaps the only distinct, feature of the

Assyrian Underworld, and they appear to supply the explanation otherwise lacking of the epithet *pulartes* given by Homer to Aïdoneus as its monarch.

In the Olympian and perhaps in other mythologies, there is a great lack of the personal ties, as among the divinities, which so powerfully unite human beings one to another. This defect becomes glaring in the Olympian system, by reason of the close resemblances it exhibits to the human forms of family and polity. But for one exception, it might almost be said that while jealousy, rivalry, contempt, and conflict abound reciprocally among them, there is no case to be found where any one deity has any personal affection for any other. The one exception, however, is conspicuous and remarkable. It is found in the relation between Apollo and Zeus. Apollo is not only the exact and constant executor of the commands of his sire, but he pays an obedience evidently founded on conformity of mind and will. This is a peculiarity so great as to be almost a solecism in the Olympian system ; and it is strongly indicative of some origin lying beyond the mere invention or experience of the Poet.

With this representation of Apollo it is difficult
to avoid comparing the great sonship of Merodach.
His is a brilliant and powerful figure, like that of
Apollo. He resembles the Apollo of general tradi-
tion, in being the champion and avenger of the gods
against Tiamat (Sayce, *Hibbert Lectures*, p. 379,
p. 101), and is so far like the Homeric Apollo,
that this conquest may very possibly be signified
in many of his characteristic epithets, and by the
punishment inflicted on Tituos for violence offered
to his mother Leto (*Od.* XI. 576-581).   To
Merodach, their first-born, the gods appeal (Sayce,
pp. 95, 320), and on him they rely.   But while
he is this to the deities at large, he is much more
than this to his primitive father Ea (p. 104) ; in
the language of Sayce, Merodach is the minister
of his counsels, the active side of his character.

There is also in Merodach another note of
correspondence with the Homeric Apollo, which
is, moreover, a note of distinction from the other
deities generally.

He is "the merciful one among the gods"
(p. 99).   At times he appears as the sun-god
(p. 101), and we have marks in the Poems that
such had been the case with Apollo : but the

general character of his attributes is philanthropic
rather than solar. Among other such marks we
find him to be, like Apollo, the god of healing
(p. 106).

He belongs to the Arcadian or pre-Semitic
system ; and in that system is the son of Ea.
Elsewhere he is affiliated to other fathers, and
this diversity is naturally consequent on the sub-
divisions of Babylonia, and the diversified and
local character of its worship. It is in later and
Assyrian times that he becomes himself Belmero-
dach, and obtains a supremacy probably due to
a local ascendency acquired by his worshippers.

Homer has drawn the formula of his trinity or
triad with much exactitude. According to the
account given by Poseidon himself (*Il.* XV. 187,
seqq.), he, Zeus, and Aïdes, are all of equal rank,
and they draw lots for their several sovereignties.
Poseidon allows to Zeus authority over his own
sons and daughters ; but claims independence for
himself : grudgingly admitting in the last resort
that Zeus has the prerogatives of a senior (*ibid.*
204-207). In the division of power, the earth,
including Olympos, remains unappropriated, or
common ground. The Babylonian triad, of Anu,

Bel, and Ea, is less precisely outlined, and in its ordinary shape does not include the Underworld. But in some forms of that mythology the lord of the ghost-world even carried the notes of supremacy. It seems probable, as the Egyptian arrangement appears much less distinct, that Homer drew his suggestion of a triad from a Babylonian source, and readjusted the particulars according to the exigencies of his Olympian system : paying off, as it were, with dignity, divinities who had elsewhere been actually supreme, but who were only represented in the nascent Hellas by influences of secondary power. This triad has all the appearance of an artificial and borrowed arrangement, inasmuch as the three have as a body no common action, and no governing authority. But it is convenient in securing for Poseidon the rank he had enjoyed as Ea ; and in placing Aïdoneus on a kind of retired list. It may also be that the arrangement, by which Homer brings the office of Aïdoneus nearly to a sinecure, may possibly have been suggested by the position of Ana or Anu, who was more a superintending than an active divinity.

I have now gone through the points in which the

present evidence of derivation from the Assyrian monuments of knowledge or ideas exhibited in the Homeric next appears to be the most clear and full. There remains, however, another class of cases deserving some notice ; inasmuch as at a number of points, the Assyrian monuments establish presumptions respecting the derivation of Homeric knowledge from that quarter, which cannot be termed more than conjectural, but which are not on that account to be cast aside at once as unreasonable.

For example, as to the observation of the stars, and the use of them as guides in navigation. Wherever we find these in Homer it is in company with foreign not Hellenic association.

The works of Hephaistos, that is to say works of art, lie outside the domestic sphere of the Achaians. Of these works the Shield of Achilles is the chief; and it is on the Shield, in its first compartment, that we have the only passage where Homer presents to us the stars as a whole together with the names of some principal stars. The coasting navigation, and those narrow seas with which the Poet's countrymen were conversant, left little scope or need for the aid of astronomical observation. But, when Odysseus has to perform his seventeen days' voyage from Ogygiè, then he receives from the foreign goddess of the island express instructions to work the course of his raft by this means (*Od.* V. 270-278). It seems clear that all such knowledge came to him from the Phœnicians, and rational if not necessary to suppose that they derived it, in their original home on the Persian Gulf, from a Chaldæan source.

I will hazard another conjecture with respect to the singularly bold conceptions which Homer formed of works of fine art. Here at least the scientific doctrine of *abiogenesis* is not applicable. In this highest branch of industry Homer distinctly assigns to the divine artist the faculty of giving actual life to its metallic products. Remark for instance the figures on the battle compartment of the Shield.

ὡμίλευν δ' ὥστε ζωοὶ βροτοί, ἠδὲ μάχοντο,
νεκρούς τ' ἀλλήλων ἔρυον κατατεθνειῶτας.[1]

Doubtless, the words are susceptible of an interpretation less daring. They might mean a mere resemblance to actual life by way of suggesting it. But they are exceptionally vivid in themselves :

[1] *Il.* XVIII. 539, 540.

and the construction I put upon them becomes I think the natural one, when it is borne in mind that Homer unquestionably ascribes automatic movement to the metallic dogs in the Palace of Alkinoos, where they fulfil the office of guards. They are also death-less, and have perpetual youth (*Od.* VII. 91-94). But further, not only the attendant figures of Hephais-tos, but even the chairs or seats which Hephaistos wrought for the Olympian assembly (*Il.* XVIII. 417-420, 313-377) had the power of automatic move-ment ; in sum, the idea of spontaneous motion was never so boldly applied as by Homer in dealing with works of art. He could hardly have been led in this direction by Egyptian art, which is successful in re-presenting rest but ineffective in dealing with motion. This idea is, I conceive, far more congenial to the art of Assyria. It seems at least possible that the wings so boldly given to gods, men, and quadrupeds, both in Assyria and to some extent in Egypt,[1] may have been the means of suggesting to Homer a further step or stride, and may have led him to endow the metallic figure itself, as it comes from the artist's hands, with the spontaneous gift ? I pass on.

Heptaism, or the systematic and significant use

[1] See Dr. Tylor in *Proceedings of the Society of Biblical Archæ-ology* for June 1890.

of the number seven, while it may be traced else-
where, is eminently and peculiarly Chaldæan.   It
appears (1) in the representation of the winds as
seven in number; (2) in the number of trans-
gressions, seven multiplied by seven ;[1] (3) in the
seven days of the Flood Legend ; (4) in the
intervals chosen for the mission of the birds from
the vessel of Hasisadra ; (5) in the number of
the rebellious spirits, described as seven ;[2] (6) in
the seven gates of the Underworld, and in a
multitude of other particulars.   Of these the most
remarkable is the number of seven heavenly
bodies, which entered profoundly into the system
of worship, so that in an Assyrian inscription we
even find the stars taking precedence of the higher
gods, of Assur and of Merodach.[3]   The only very
marked use of the number seven in Homer is as
to the city of Thebes ; and the name of that city
appears to be not of Assyrian but of Egyptian
origin.   The two currents, however, joined, and
formed as it were a common pool, when they

---

[1] Manual published by the Society for promoting Christian
Knowledge, pp. 27, 28.

[2] Smith's *Assyrian Discoveries*, pp. 400-402 ; Sayce, *Hibbert Lec-
tures*, p. 82.

[3] Sayce, p. 403.

reached Phœnicia and her ships ; so that Homer may have derived much, both from the one country and the other, without knowing in each instance to which of them it was that he owed his information.

A conjecture of Assyrian derivation may again be hazarded in connection with the twenty seats which Hephaistos is engaged in fabricating for the gods of the Olympian assembly, at the time when Thetis visits him for the grand purpose of replacing the lost arms of Achilles.

These seats, endowed with the power of automatic motion, were (*eeikosi pantes*) twenty in number. The Poet's numerical ideas were commonly vague, and we have no exact means of determining the number of his Olympian deities. The religion of the country was still in a state of fluxion, and there are one or two divinities of doubtful title. But upon the whole, as I have already shown (*Sup*. Sect. III., XIV., and XVIII.), the number of those who had seats in the ordinary Olympian meetings seems to have been about or nearly twenty. So again in Assyria we have no means of designating with confidence a particular number for the members of the Thearchy, whereas, as in the case of the Romans, we describe them by the name of the twelve *Dî majores.* Canon Rawlinson, however, has touched this subject in his *Religions of the World*, p. 18, and he notices the existence of eight great gods, six of their wives, and five astral gods. It seems probable that the number twenty may have been suggested from this source, with a vagueness strange to us, but by no means alien to the manner of Homer.

A fourth case of possible suggestion is offered by the curious representation of the effect produced on earth by the descent of Ishtar to Hades. It was a general disorganisation, caused by the absence of a ruling deity from her proper sphere. "The master ceases from commanding, the slave from obeying" (Rawlinson, p. 25). Does it not seem possible that some form of this legend may have suggested to the Poet the bold threat of Helios in the *Odyssey*, XII. 381, that unless due respect is paid to his demands for redress, he will not rise next morning as usual upon gods and men, but will shine in the Underworld?

Again, the story of the Flood has a conspicuous place among the Babylonian legends, and

was the first among the discoveries to challenge
a large share of public attention in this country.
The chief interest attaching to it lies in its rela-
tion to the account given in Genesis.[1] In Homer
there is but one, and that not an unequivocal
trace of this tradition.   It is conveyed in the
form of a simile, where he compares the motion of
Trojan horses at full speed to a flood sent by
Zeus upon a land to punish the iniquities of evil
rulers. · The pointed nature of this connection
between a great inundation and the offences of
men renders it probable that the Poet was
acquainted with some legend such as could
supply a basis for it.   I suppose it was little
likely that he could draw this information from
the valley of the Nile ; where indeed the swelling
of the waters was familiarly known, not, however,
as a retributive visitation, but as a blessing, and
indeed a necessity.   It seems then reasonable to
suppose that the knowledge which suggested the
simile came from the same source as that which
supplied the Tablets of Nineveh.

Lastly.   It has to be observed that the Helios
of Homer is furnished with a patronymic.   He is

---

[1] Mr. George Smith, *Assyrian Discoveries*, p. 188 *seqq.*

Eslios Huperion ; but this epithet is not given I think except in cases outside the familiar Greek tradition, as in *Il.* VIII. 480, and again in the *Odyssey,* I. 3, and XII. 176 ; both of these last being cases where the scene is laid in the Outer Zone, and in a part of it where the Sun is the working head of the Thearchy. Now in the Babylonian system also the Sun had a Father. The Sungod was the offspring of the Moongod. The particular form of this arrangement was obviously one which, as 'Sayce observes (*Hibbert Lectures,* p. 155), could only prevail where the Moongod was, as in one form of the Babylonian system, the supreme object of worship.

THE END

Printed by R. & R. CLARK, *Edinburgh*